ANGELS
IN
RED
SUSPENDERS

Radio Broadcasting for Developing Nations
The Gift of Story
Through Rose-colored Bifocals
This United Church of Ours
Commonsense Christianity
Is This Your Idea of a Good Time, God?
God for Beginners
Living God's Way
The Family Story Bible
Man to Man
How to Write and Publish Your Church History
Sermon Seasonings

RALPH MILTON

ANGELS
IN
RED
SUSPENDERS

Northstone

Editor: Michael Schwartzentruber
Cover design: Lois Huey-Heck, Margaret Kyle
Front cover angel: public domain
Back cover: Kent Lindsey Photography
Interior design: Margaret Kyle, Julie Bachewich
Consulting art director: Robert MacDonald

Northstone Publishing Inc. is an employee-owned company, committed to caring
for the environment and all creation. Northstone recycles, reuses
and composts, and encourages readers to do the same. Resources are printed on
recycled paper and more environmentally friendly groundwood papers (newsprint),
whenever possible. The trees used are replaced through
donations to the Scoutrees For Canada Program.
Ten percent of all profit is donated to charitable organizations.

Canadian Cataloguing in Publication Data
Milton, Ralph
Angels in Red Suspenders
ISBN 1-896836-10-0
1. Christian life—Anecdotes. 2. Christian life—Humor.
3. Canadian wit and humor (English)* I. Title.
BV4517.M54 1997   248.4   C97-910439-4

Published by Northstone Publishing Inc.

Printing
9 8 7 6 5 4 3 2 1

Printed in Canada by
Transcontinental Printing Inc.
Peterborough, Ontario

To the loving memory
our son
Jeremy Lloyd

Contents

We Can Fly! • 17

Laughing with God • 59

The Meaning of It All • 87

How to Sleep through a Sermon • 127

The Whole World in God's Hands • 153

The Gender Wars • 193

Grow Old along with Me • 215

The Time of Our Lives • 243

Foreword

LAUGHTER AND TEARS

a few words about what to expect in this strange book...

Laughter is good therapy. So is crying. I really hope this book makes you laugh occasionally. Cry sometimes too. But I hope you'll do more laughing than crying.

Sometimes, I hope, my experiences will touch yours and bring a smile to your lips or a catch in your throat. When that happens to us, we grow a little inside. If we suppress the laughter or the tears, we die a little each time.

A big part of this book is about laughter. It is a celebration of life. I may be the last optimist alive, but I insist on taking a positive attitude toward life. For the most part. Once in awhile I lapse into searing sarcasm and anger. But mostly it is laughter – laughter that lives in the context of tears. Laughter that comes through pain. So the first thing I need to do is to tell you of the pain that I feel most intensely right now.

If you read this book all the way through, you'll discover that life has not always been a rose garden for Bev and me and our family, especially recently. We suffered the tragic loss of our son Lloyd a few months before this book saw its final form. And the book is dedicated to his memory, for a very good reason.

On the shelf above my computer, I have a taxi meter. It is one of those old-fashioned kinds you don't see in cabs anymore, complete with the wind-up knob and the VACANT flag that pulls down to start the meter running.

It was a Christmas gift from Lloyd and I shall always treasure it, because it reminds me of his deep sense of humor that would bubble up and brighten the room whenever he would let it. Lloyd thought the taxi meter would be fun to put on my desk at work, and when people came in to see me I could "put them at their ease" by pulling the flag down and have the thing ticking loudly and counting up the dollars.

Bev and I fondly remember summers at Naramata Center in the Okanagan Valley, when he and the other children would spend hours working out and rehearsing the most astonishing and usually quite awful routines for skit night. All of us would groan and Lloyd would grin.

That kind of humor happened less and less in his last years, but the memory of that impish smile at a really bad joke or outrageous pun is something I will treasure always. And it is a legacy he leaves for me – a legacy that is, I hope, reflected in this book.

Humor was one of the many gifts that, because of his terrible, painful start in life, never flowered. I think it might have flowered, if he had not lived his first two years in the hell of a desperately dysfunctional foster home.

So the book is dedicated as much to what might have been, as to what was.

• • •

Partly because of that, I need to laugh with you and cry with you. Laughter and tears come from the same place in our soul. Laughter and tears wash the soul so that it may heal. Most of us already know that tears work that way, but deep and genuine laughter does the same kind of thing.

In my life, and perhaps in yours, there's been a heavy dose of personal tragedy lately. A glance at the news media, and we know the reality of world tragedy as well. It often seems there's nothing to laugh about. Only tears are appropriate. But I say laughter needs to be there within the tears, now more than ever, or the tears will turn into despair.

You could call it "fiddling while Rome burns."

Putting time and effort into a book like this while the nation's economy is shuddering, Third World people are getting poorer, the atomic powers still hoard their nuclear stockpiles, and we are grieving over the loss of a son we love ... well, the kindest thing you could call it would be "irresponsible." And yet...

I remember a church service, years ago. The ushers had just taken up the offering. They were walking down the aisle when one of them tripped on the pile in the carpet, and sent his offering plates and those of the other usher flying in a flurry of envelopes, dollar bills and quarters all over the front of the church.

The congregation sat in stunned silence.

Then the minister said the only thing that could be said. "For goodness sake, laugh."

And they did.

Till the tears rolled down their faces. And while they laughed, they got down on their hands and knees and picked up the money, put it back on the offering plates, and carried on with the worship service.

The world has always been in trouble. It may be in more trouble now than ever, but trouble is not a new thing for the human species.

There are at least two ways to react.

One way is to be so solemn about everything that you never laugh at all. It makes good sense, which is why the early Quakers tried it. "Life is tragic," they said, "therefore nobody will laugh." It's a reasonable response.

The other position is to laugh at almost everything, on the theory that the laughing, while it doesn't solve the problem, does at least put it into perspective. It's a bit like praying.

Our family's grief is deep and terrible. But sometimes in the grieving we remember Lloyd's delightful humor – sometimes I look up at that old taxi meter – and we can laugh a little through our anger and our tears.

We don't laugh to deny the magnitude of grief. We don't laugh to avoid the pain. We laugh, because not to do so would deny the beauty and the joy of a young man we loved. It would deny the loss we were grieving.

I've said it so often, my friends are getting tired of hearing me. Laughter is not the opposite of seriousness. Laughter is the opposite of despair.

One of the common traits of dictators, revolutionaries, church bureaucrats and television evangelists, is that they are afraid to laugh at themselves. Laughter might reveal their humanity and uncover their nakedness.

Of course we must rage and protest at the danger and the injustice. The work we have to do, the call we hear, is about serious issues. But serious is different from solemn.

Children are naturally serious, but they are hardly ever solemn. I'm learning that again from Jake and Zoë, my grandchildren. They undertake life with intensity and passion, and involve themselves totally in whatever is happening to themselves or those around them. That involves laughing and crying and feeling anger and love and joy and sadness.

But Zoë and Jake hardly ever put on the adult mask of solemnity which turns out to be a very sophisticated way of ducking reality.

Humor is very serious. But it is hardly ever solemn.

Humor, rather, should be defined by people like Tevya in the musical *Fiddler on the Roof*. When the peasant Jews are being expelled from their homes in Russia, one villager says, "Anatevka hasn't been exactly the Garden of Eden." The Rabbi observes that their people "have been forced out of many places at a moment's notice."

"Maybe," quips Tevya, "that's why we always wear our hats."

Maybe that's why Jewish people are still around to tell their stories. "Tears dipped in honey," a friend once called it.

Jesus was a Jew who lived when times were at least as bad as they are now. He used wild hyperbole and wry humor, as much as he used cries of outrage, to confront the powers and principalities.

Leo Tolstoy, who also lived in a time of turmoil, put it this way:

If someone were to tell me that it lay in my power to write a novel explaining every social question from a particular viewpoint that I believed to be the correct one, I still wouldn't spend two hours on it.

But if I were told that what I am writing will be read...by the children of today, and that those children will laugh, weep and learn to love life as they read, why then I would devote the whole of my life and energy to it.

Tolstoy I am not. But the gift of humor and the gift of tears are sometimes mine. And if the articles that follow in this book help a few of us to "laugh, weep and learn to love life" while we confront the evil that threatens our world, why then that is reason enough for writing them.

Don't expect what follows to be comprehensive or consistent. Consistency is not a value I hold very highly for the simple reason that what is true on one occasion, or for one person, may not be true on another occasion or for another person. So a number of things in this book will be quite contradictory and all of them may be true. Or false. Most likely a little of both.

Don't expect a full-blown philosophy of life in these pages. I really don't know if I have one, but if I did, I wouldn't have the nerve to lay it on you. And if you picked up this book looking for solutions or formulas, well, I'm sorry. I don't believe in neat solutions and formulas because I don't think they work.

These essays are insights. Flashes of light that have come to me as I have lived through the life that has come my way. When I have presented these yarns, insights, reflections during various seminars, workshops and speeches, enough people have told me they found them helpful that I feel I must share them in this form.

Some of the essays have no function except to make you giggle a little. Occasionally you'll realize I'm pulling your leg. There are those who say I'm given to hyperbole, but I never, ever exaggerate, under any circumstances, though sometimes I get a bit excited.

Sometimes, in these searchings of my own soul, I may touch the tender places in yours, and perhaps bring a tear, a memory or an insight. I hope for nothing more. I'm not trying to convince you or convert you nor do I even expect to be taken seriously most of the time. What I have in my head and my heart is laid out here, and if you find anything that fits, that's wonderful. If not, that's okay too.

These essays are arranged more according to mood and content than chronologically. I have made no particular effort to update the ages of my grandchildren, Jake and Zoë who have taught me so much, nor bring up to date some other references. None of those time indicators are important anyway.

There are other characters in the haphazard human drama you'll find laid out on these pages. There's Bev, my partner and spouse and friend of almost 40 years, and Jim Taylor my colleague and friend whom I have worked with and argued with for several decades.

There's Grace, Lloyd's twin sister, and Kari (my daughter) and Don who are Jake and Zoë's mom and dad, and Mark my eldest son.

And lots of treasured friends and extended family whose names are sometimes given and sometimes changed to protect the guilty.

The essays were written under varying circumstances and in many moods. If you've read some of my other stuff, you may recognize a few of the pieces that have been recycled from other publications such as *Aha!!!* (a preaching journal for clergy) and previous books, especially *Through Rose Colored Bifocals* which has been out of print for years. Most of the stuff here has never been printed before, though much of it has been used in seminars and speeches.

I hope the book is, in some small way, a blessing to you, the way the writing of it has brought some healing to me.

Ralph Milton
Kelowna, BC, 1997

We Can Fly!

Why Angels Can Fly

I am an angel.

That's a bit of a stretch, I know. A guy with a beard and red suspenders is definitely not the first image that pops into your mind when you think of angels. You think of those fat, five-year-old cherubs that Raphael put in his paintings, or St. Michael who looks like the Pope with wings. But a large-nosed, flat-footed, past-his-prime male in blue jeans and bifocals...?

So expand your mind. Broaden your vision. Use your imagination. Take another look at that photo on the back cover. That's me, and I'm an angel. Red suspenders are part of my angel outfit.

Red suspenders are Jake's favorite. Jake and his sister, Zoë, (my grandkids) are angels too, even though their mom and dad (who are also angels) doubt that occasionally. Everybody calls cute kids "angels."

It's been a while since anybody called *me* an angel. "Old devil" is more likely, and describes me just as accurately as "angel." I could write an essay twice as long as this one about the times I've screwed up or even been fundamentally evil.

I know that. You know that. Let's leave it at that. Besides, lots of religious traditions have bad angels in them, including the Christian tradition. Never try to typecast us angels.

Jake likes the red suspenders because he can pull them as far as they go and let them snap back onto my belly. I overreact with great, grandfatherly noises and Jake giggles. It's the kind of game angels play with each other. Angels like fun that requires no intelligence but does require two people who love each other. The love is what makes the game work. It's the love that makes us ordinary humans, angels.

I learned about angels reading a book by Rabbi Harold Kushner. In *When Bad Things Happen to Good People*, Rabbi Kushner has a wonderful fantasy about one of the creation legends in the Bible.

Jews believe in just one God. That was really important to the folks who collected the stories that went into the Bible. In that creation legend Rabbi Kushner is talking about, God makes the world and all the plants and animals and birds and bugs. Then God says, "Let us create humans in our image…" "*Us?*" "*Our* image…?" Who is God talking to in that legend, if the world has just been created and there is only one God and no people yet?

The good rabbi grins and says it must be the animals. God looks at the animals and says, "Let us make humans in *our* image – like you animals, and like me, God."

Biblical scholars had a cerebral hernia when the rabbi proposed that one, but who cares. It's a delightful idea – so delightful it *must* be true.

That's how I found out I was an angel. Angels are not as wonderful as God but a whole lot more wonderful than animals.

So if I, as a human, bear the characteristics of both my Creator and of a crawfish – 50 percent God and 50 percent gorilla, – the God part must be a little bit angelic, wouldn't you think? Tradition has it that when God becomes visible to humans, it's as an angel. And I am certainly visible. (My doctor would like me to be about 40 pounds less visible.)

The angel part doesn't show all the time, of course. Not even most of the time. But sometimes. Sometimes I am angelic. Yes, believe it.

So are you.

When you and I are loving, the angel vibrations are turned up to "high." When Zoë snuggles down into my arms, and I sit there in the rocker feeling content as a cow in a cornfield, both Zoë and I are angels.

When I do something good for someone else, or when I let someone else do something good to me, I am being an angel.

What's so unusual about that? Nothing at all. It means you are an angel and so is everybody else. At least sometimes.

I have a friend who is a cabinet minister in a provincial government. I believe he is doing his level best to be as just and caring and fair as he can be in the thankless political arena. When he's doing his selfless best, he's an angel. When Louise next door brings over a tray of hot muffins, she is an angel.

A few years ago, I came across a very confused woman sitting on the curb, after midnight, in her nightgown. She was disoriented and cold and badly in need of help. A few hours later in the hospital she said to me, "You're an angel."

"Naw!" I said. But she was right. I was. And so was she, because in her confusion and extreme vulnerability, she brought out some of the best in me. I don't see that good part of me very often because I am so busy being important. There's an old tradition that tells us to pay attention to folks like that woman, because you never know when you might be encountering an "angel unawares."

There are no really clear divisions. Imagine a line with God at one end and an amoeba at the other. In between you have, just below God, angels, humans, mammals, lower orders of animals, insects, and all the other tiny creepy crawlies that make up this exciting universe till you get to that amoeba.

The divisions are relatively clear at the bottom end, but at the top where you find God – angel – human, it is not clear where one ends and another begins. If you go digging around through the world's religious literature, that just fuzzifies things.

In my own Judeo-Christian tradition, the word "angel" comes from the Greek *angelos* which at first simply meant "messenger." The older Hebrew term, *mal'ak* basically means the same thing. In other words, whoever God uses to get in touch with us, that's an angel. My experience tells me that most often God communicates to me through other people. Occasionally people have told me they feel God has communicated to them through me. That makes us all angels.

All the world's religious traditions have that wisdom about the divine nature of humans. The *Bhagavad-Gita* says, "The supreme Self...dwells in every creature." Sikhism asks us to recognize God "within yourself." Islam tells us that God's "soul whispers within" us and that God is nearer to us "than the jugular vein."

My ideas about angels are old ideas that have been bopping around the heads of saints and seers for thousands of years. There's something wonderfully divine about us humans when we are at our best; that's when we become God's messengers. Angels. And something frighteningly diabolical when we are at our worst. And then, also, we are angels, because traditionally, angels are not always good and sweet and wonderful. In the Judeo-Christian tradition, there are evil angels as well. And sometimes the bad angels and the good angels are the same people.

I heard a story about a teacher who asked the children, "If all the bad people were painted red and all the good people were painted green, what color would you be?"

"Striped," answered one very wise child.

I'm talking about the green stripes in this book, mostly – the times when we're acting out of the God side of our humanity – when we're dressed up in wings and halos. It is true that underneath that angel outfit we wear a suit of red underwear, and the thing that keeps the halo from sliding off are the horns underneath. We'd better not forget that.

One way to tell the difference between good angels and not-good angels is that the good angels love to laugh. Angel laughter is a very special kind of laughter. It's the kind of laughter I get from Jake when he snaps my red suspenders. It's the kind of chortle I get from Zoë when I make rude noises with my lips on her neck. It's the laughter of pure joy – of love that is not deserved or earned but simply given and received.

That's why angels can fly. Even flat-footed, gray-bearded, bifocaled, red-suspendered angels.

We can fly because we take ourselves lightly.

Everybody's Happy

You've heard the classic children's joke.

Question: Why do firefighters wear red suspenders?

Answer: To keep their pants up.

If you are six or seven years old, that is really very funny.

Not a lot of people ask, "Why does Ralph wear red suspenders?" but when they do, I tell them about an angel named Spiro, and a time when I was being not exactly angelic, and how red suspenders brought peace, joy and happiness to my little corner of the world.

I have an annoying nerve problem in my leg. When it hurts, which is often, I get cranky and become a pain in the *patusche*. I go to the nerve specialist and the bone specialist and the muscle specialist and the general specialist and they all look very wise and tell me, "It's not life-threatening..."

I already know that. I want them to stop the pain which isn't severe but is persistent – a burr under my saddle. And it gets me feeling pretty growly.

I start experimenting to relieve the pain. Baggy pants, I discover, help. But to get them baggy enough I buy a size too large, then have the waist taken in. I take the pants to Spiro who has a tailor shop above one of the stores downtown. It's full of sewing machines and ironing boards and 1950s pinups of semi-nude women with their navels airbrushed away. This time I go to see Spiro with a pair of blue jeans.

"Cannot fix blue jean," says Spiro, standing underneath a sign that says, "No alterations too difficult." He is a kind and gentle man who understands about my leg and wants to help. "Zewing machine needle all go ping, ping, ping on blue jean," he says. "Why not you go buy zum zoospenders. Zoospenders better for holding pants than belt."

Spiro is an angel. At least, the part of him that wants to help a man with a hurting leg – that part is angelic. Spiro gives me a pat on the back and sends me off to a store that sells working clothes, and there I buy my first suspenders since high school.

In the small town of Horndean where I grew up, all the men and boys wore suspenders. When I went off to Winnipeg to school, I knew right away that real city guys wore belts. Nothing was more important to teenage me than being cool, so I bought belts and wore them all those years till I encountered Spiro.

They only have red suspenders at that store, so I buy red suspenders and take them home and clip them to my trousers.

Liberation! Freedom! I haven't been this comfortable since I was 12 years old. Thank you, Spiro! You are an angel!

Why did I wear a belt all those years? Half a century of suffering! Why does any male, anywhere, anytime, ever wear a belt? Suspenders are 99.9 percent more comfortable than belts. You can breathe! You can sit down and your belt buckle doesn't mash your belly button. You can bend over and your buns don't display a "plumber's cleavage." As for that nerve in my leg – well it still hurts, but only half as much. And only sometimes. Spiro was more helpful than all those specialists.

I have been a "men's libber" for years, even writing a book (*Man to Man*) as a resource for the men's movement. I stand there, half-naked in front of my closet, with a handful of those hateful belts and wonder why I and others of my sex wear those gut-binding tourniquets around our middles. Who decrees that men should suffer so for the sake of a waistline?

Okay, so we do it to ourselves. Now's the time to stop it!

Do you remember, at the height of the feminist movement, the sisters had a "bra burning"? They decided it was better to be comfortable than to conform to somebody else's idea of sexy.

So now it's the men's turn, I figure. I become a born-again belt-basher, and try to organize a rally at which all my liberated male friends will burn their belts in a great bonfire, and put on suspenders as a symbol of our new-found freedom.

"Men of the world unite! You have nothing to lose but your waistlines!"

"Give it a rest!" say my friends of both sexes when I get evangelical about suspenders. So far not many converts. None, actually. Being a born-again braces believer only manages to get me bemused looks from friends and colleagues who try very hard to say nice things.

Except Jake. He wears suspenders sometimes, but then a two-year-old doesn't have a whole lot of choice when his granddad is dressing him.

"Make a virtue out of necessity, Ralph," I think. So I assume a superior, long-suffering look, and buy six pairs of red suspenders. Red suspenders become a personal trademark.

There are other benefits. Red suspenders are just mildly ridiculous, which gives folks a chance to laugh a little, and that helps sometimes.

I got liberated from belts and became a born-again suspender person about the time I got elected to a fairly prestigious position in the church – as close as my denomination gets to a bishop.

"Dad? A Bishop?" My kids are just a bit incredulous. So are my friends, and some avoid me or try to think of something "religious" to say. People often get uptight when church potentates show up anywhere, and everybody tries to clean up their language and nobody ever offers you a drink of anything except tea or lemonade.

When I wear red suspenders it lightens everything up. They realize I'm just as rotten, depraved, confused, ignorant and generally messed-up as they are.

I also get to be comfortable. My leg doesn't hurt as much. My host breaks out a bottle of wine. My publisher gets a good title for this book.

Everybody's happy!

Dancing the Rubber Ice

Am I just sentimental? Or is it true that spring on the prairies is more passionate and fun?

I live in the Okanagan Valley now, where springtime kind of seeps in slowly underneath the door. On the prairies, springtime comes like that! BAM! You shovel out a snowstorm one day, and the next there's balm upon the breeze. The swift seduction of a prairie spring sweeps you away with a warm and passionate kiss – loves you quickly into summer and is gone. A short, surprising love-affair with life.

When spring hits the prairies, it thaws. Wow! Does it thaw! The sloughs fill up and the ditches run full, and children quickly trade their winter long johns for gum boots and go looking for rubber ice to dance on.

Do you know what rubber ice is?

It only happens in a slough or a hollow where the water is exactly one inch deeper than a nine-year-old boy's rubber boots. It happens overnight. A thin, plastic layer – not like ordinary ice. Rubber ice is flexible and, well, rubbery.

Adults have no idea what to do with rubber ice. But a child knows. You have to dance it.

• • •

I am nine years old and I can dance. One slow and lingering step and I can feel the ice sink slightly, sending snaps and crackles detonating through the slough. I have nine-year-old skill and nine-year-old rhythm, and the keen mind I lost when puberty came with its new kinds of challenges.

I am nine and I know this dance. I test the ice with each slow step, and know exactly when to move just as the ice begins to crack. Quickly, not too fast, a gliding slow ballet – always moving forward because to stop, even for a second, is to break the ice. Nor can you go back to ice you've danced before because it is weak. But there is always lots of future – lots of ice to draw you on, dancing, moving forward just at the moment when the ice begins to sink beneath your feet.

I get a little braver – stay a little longer in each spot. My dance slows as I dare the ice to break, push the edges of my spring-time passion, test the boundaries of my boyhood.

And the ice will break. Eventually, it always does. And I run, wet and shivering and defeated to my mom, who dries me off and scolds me softly and talks about pneumonia.

"Aw, mom, my feet aren't even a teensy bit cold. It's boiling out there."

There is gentleness in mother's scolding. And sometimes just a hint of laughter. I think maybe mom remembers rubber ice when she was nine.

• • •

Spring on the prairies is a quick, passionate affair with life. Rubber ice to dance on, swimming holes to freeze in, feet to go barefoot on. Then spring is gone and the hot summer is upon us. Time to get to work. Time to live a thing called hope.

Those who farm the dry and unforgiving prairies know about hope.

Yes, hope.

Not bloody-minded positive thinking. Not gritting your teeth and toughing it out till the economy improves. Not even opti-mism. It's embracing the glory, the passion of life, and accepting the crud that infects it. And the pain. Springtime has taught you that you will break through and your boots will fill up – but not to dance the ice is to deny the gift of life with all its pleasure and its passion and its pain. To refuse the springtime teaching of rub-ber ice is to say "no" to summer hope.

Hope, real hope, is deeper than mere optimism. It's not at all like cranking up a positive attitude. It's not the phony "power-think" of real estate sales people. There's nothing "Pollyanna" about it. You can't describe hope, or teach it, but you can see it sometimes, and you can live it.

I've seen hope in the swollen belly of my daughter when she bore our grandchild. I've seen hope in the face of a tired street worker showing a broken woman where she can get a bit of rest, a sense of safety and a shower. I've seen hope in the eyes of a friend dying from cancer – convinced her life would not end when her body died. I've seen hope in the wrinkled face of my grandmother who lay on her bed and told me, "I'm just waiting for my Jesus."

I experience hope every time I plant a seed or tell a story to my grandchild or sit with Bev, my mate of almost 40 years, and hold her hand and listen to the heartbeat of our life, and remember how we've danced the rubber ice together.

I know about hope because as a small boy I learned to dance the rubber ice and feel the passion of a prairie springtime. And I found a "mom" that I could run to in my prayers – a Mother who danced the rubber ice and showed me something of the face of God.

Of Lullabies and Peach Fuzz

My mother sang me lullabies. My father didn't.

I remembered that one day, driving in the car, hearing Maureen Forrester sing a lullaby on the radio.

I remembered singing lullabies to my own children. And reading them stories.

I wish my father had sung me lullabies, too, because then he might have known some of the sensual, holy joy of a child close to your body, a child drawing strength and giving hope. And I might have known that God could also be a man as well as woman.

Not long ago I watched friends put a child to bed with a record of some lullabies. "It's better than my croaky voice," she said.

No!

Canned lullabies are half-hearted imitations of the truth, like canned peaches eaten from a bowl that offer pale and one-dimensional memories of a hot and buzzing orchard, and of an August peach, red and warm from sun blessed tree, juice dribbling down your beard, the taste and smell of summer life flowing through your soul.

The sound of a lullaby is all you get on tape. It may be better music. But it's music for the ears and not the soul.

It is not the music of a father's heartbeat, nor the warmth of body, nor the smell of woman. It is not the sense of oneness with another, with creation, with the future, with a child.

Canned peaches have the smell of summer sterilized away – no leaves that rustle in the breeze, no blemishes, no itchy fuzz, no inkling of eternity.

Food. But no spiritual nutrition.

God can't speak in words. God speaks to us in life... in the sweetness of an orchard peach, in the taste of mother love, in the texture of a father's tenderness.

Carnal knowledge of an orchard peach, or of a baby lullabied, is the pulse of holiness.

We Can Fly

Whenever they chose up sides for anything, I was always chosen last.

That was partly because my dad was the principal of the school and partly because I was no good at anything that mattered. I yearned, ached, longed to be popular with the other kids in our town. I would have sold my soul to anyone who could have found me a way not to be chosen last for soccer or baseball or whatever.

It didn't help that I grew too fast. My nickname changed from Slug to Slim, and my mind no longer knew the length of my limbs. I developed a stoop, which I still have, trying to get down to the size of my school mates. I was the most awkward kid in town. I literally tripped over the design on the kitchen linoleum.

I had no talent to invest in anything. Thirteen years old and already a failure. I spent hours in my room writing poems and stories. My mom liked my stories. "You've got talent," she said. What do mothers know?

In grade 11, Miss Thompson, my English teacher, liked my stories and my essays. And I got an A+ in English which qualified me as a genuine "twerp." ("Nerd" was not in our vocabulary at that time.) I liked to sing too, but that got me even less status than writing.

That was almost half a century ago. Now my classmates are in various states of decrepitude (as I am) and their athletic abilities have disappeared as have their waistlines. But I write better now and enjoy it more than ever, and music gives me more pleasure each year. Mother and Miss Thompson were right. There is some use for those talents after all.

There's an old creation legend that the birds felt they'd been cheated when they looked at their wings.

"What can you do with these things?" they asked God. "You can't walk with them. You can't pick things up. Wings are ugly and awkward to carry around."

"You can fly," said God.

"Fly? Whadaya mean, fly? What's fly?" the birds demanded.

"Spread them out as wide as you can. Way out wide. Now move them up and down. Harder. Now see, they lift you from the ground. You can fly! You can fly!"

Reality Check

A few months ago, I went into one of those boutique type of stores in a tourist area where they sell overpriced clothing to gullible visitors. I never buy stuff in stores like that, of course.

But they had a nice sweatshirt – my size. It was a soft beige with a bull moose embroidered in brown thread. It had class! When I tried it on the very young, very feminine sales person said, "Oooh, sexy!" I believed her. Don't ask how much I paid.

I wore my trendy new sweatshirt when I went to visit my grandkids.

"I like your shirt, Dad," said Kari, my daughter.

I picked up grandson Jake to get my hug. A small finger touched the symbol of masculine virility embroidered on my breast.

"Cow!" said Jake.

Reality check.

Some years ago I was in the office of George Rodgers, a leading church person in Edmonton. George wasn't there, but his nine-year-old son Mark was with me.

On the wall of his office was a photo of George shaking hands with the Pope. "Who's that?" I asked Mark, wondering if he knew the famous person his dad was talking to.

Mark knew who was famous in his life. "I don't know who that guy is," said Mark. Then with obvious pride. "But that's my dad!"

Reality check.

I have just been reading some letters written by colleagues about me. The letters say some really complimentary things and I am moved, delighted, flattered. I walk around the house – my ego inflated, full to bursting – wondering if my family know what a fine and wonderful person they have living with them.

I pick up Zoë. She grins at her Grandpa, just to let me know she loves me, then gives my beard a solid tug.

Reality check.

And just to make sure all the air is out, Zoë grabs my nose and gives it a vigorous twist.

God must have a sense of humor. Who else but a laughing God sends children to teach us reality?

Who Would Believe It?

Years ago, my parents lived in the Tuxedo area, not far from the Winnipeg zoo. One day Mom was looking out the window.

"Henry," she said, "there's a buffalo on our front lawn."

Dad was understandably skeptical. "Are you all right, Marie?"

"Of course I'm all right," she said. "I'm telling you there's a buffalo on our front lawn."

And there was!

It was a big, buffalo bull and it had escaped from the zoo. But for awhile, Dad wondered if Mom had flipped her lid. It was too crazy to believe, but there it was, munching on his grass.

Years later in Calgary, we had a bunch of hot air balloons floating over the city. There was some kind of competition or convention, or whatever it is when hot-air balloonists get together to go ballooning.

But balloonists, it seems, are not always totally sure where they are going to land. (All of this sounds like a wonderful, though undeveloped metaphor for some of the conferences and conventions I've been to.)

"Mom, Mom, come look!" shouted a five-year-old who lived just down the street from us. "There's a balloon in our back yard!"

His mom knew her five-year-old tended to have a vivid imagination. "Yes, I'm sure there is, Eric," she said, and kept right on with her work.

"No, Mom, really. Honest! There is a big red and yellow balloon in our back yard."

And there was!

Balloons and buffaloes in people's yards are too improbable to believe. But sometimes they are true.

A God head over heals in love with creation is too improbable to believe. But women who gaze out of the narrow windows of life will believe. So will children dreaming in their back yards.

And who knows, maybe even an aging, jaded writer.

Playing Dressup

I can't help it.

I keep having these fantasies.

I play "what if" in my head. I have ideas that would solve all the problems of the world if anybody ever took me seriously.

Nobody ever does.

I have this fantasy about the world leaders playing dressup for awhile before each international conference, seeing the child in each other, and then sitting down at the negotiating table, with their costumes still on. If Bill Clinton was dressed up like Pagliacci and Boris Yeltsin like Charlie Chaplin, a whole lot of power issues would seem very insignificant and they might be able to get down to the real questions facing our world.

A fantasy a bit like that actually happened a few summers ago during a vacation. Bev and I went with six friends to Ashland, Oregon, where they do plays. Mostly Shakespeare.

They have a bunch of theaters which are full most of the year. The production and acting are first-rate. We saw six plays in six days. Cultural OD.

I have no idea how many professional people are employed doing all that serious theater in Ashland, but one of them, at least, has the soul a child.

There is a theater museum in Ashland. It's very edifying, though a bit boring. Right in the middle of all those terribly important theatrical artifacts and serious displays is one room for the children. Adult children. In the case of our little group, every one of us kids had lived more than half a century.

That children's room is full of costumes. And stage props. And hats. And really neat stuff you can do anything you want with. You can take all those costumes off the pegs and put them on and pose for pictures and pretend that you are Henry VIII or the Hag of the Bog, or Catherine the Great, or Genghis Khan or someone you just made up.

Bev and I have a photo in which I'm dressed up like a somewhat dilapidated Sir Walter Raleigh. Bev looks (she doesn't think so!) like Queen Elizabeth reading the tabloids about her kids and saying, "We are not amused."

The eight of us playing dressup were all "professional" folk – four clergy of two denominations and considerable stature included. And we were all acting like six-year-olds.

It was marvelous.

It was therapeutic.

It was holy.

Yes it was. In a profound way I don't really understand it was a deeply spiritual experience. We allowed ourselves to be children for awhile, and caught a glimpse of the center of our souls where laughter and joy and love still live – where God lives.

Six old kids and God having the time of our lives.

Boris and Bill and even Queen Elizabeth, should have been there.

Do Gerbils Go to Heaven?

The first death in our family that really meant anything to the kids happened during our sojourn in Teaneck, New Jersey. The deceased was a gerbil named Hercules. Herc for short. I had picked Herc up in my hand. He bit me, then he died. There are various theories in our family about why that may have happened, none of which I find very flattering.

Bev was worried that Herc might have had rabies. It was a reasonable worry, because we'd just come back from living in the Philippines where rabies is a terrible threat.

So Herc didn't get a dignified burial in the backyard – Herc was placed in a clear plastic bag in the freezer until we could find where you take a gerbil cadaver to be tested.

The next day, Colin, from next door, was helping us clean up after joining us for lunch. He gave up trying to find a diplomatic way to ask, and finally blurted out, "Why do you have a frozen rat in your fridge?"

It was the kids who talked most about Herc, and what his death really meant.

"Can Herc go to heaven if he's still frozen in the fridge?"

"Gerbils don't go to heaven, dummy."

"But I want Herc to go to heaven, so I can play with him again."

"Are there angels and harps and stuff like that in heaven, Dad?"

"When you get dead, you're just dead. Your body gets rotten. 'The worms crawl in, the worms crawl out, the worms play pinochle on your snout...'"

"Yuk! Dad, make him stop!"

"Will we go to heaven when we die, Dad? Angie says our whole family will all go to hell where it's hot and burning because we're Presbyterians and not Pentecostals."

Certainly, it was a "teaching moment," when Dad (me) should have offered wisdom and understanding. Not remembering what I said, I can't say if I offered either. But I've remembered that little "childish" conversation because in it you can find just about all the questions around death and resurrection that still bug us as adults.

That all happened a couple of decades ago. Today, the questions in my mind, the questions articulated by my friends, are the same ones my kids asked, even though the words we use sound more sophisticated.

"What happens when I die? Will my friends or family be there? Are there really streets of gold, and harps, and angels, and St. Peter guarding the pearly gates? Have I chosen the right religion, and will God kick me out if I chose wrong? Will I go to hell if I've done some bad things?"

I don't know if I gave much of an answer to my kids way back then, and I know I don't have any neat answers to those adult questions now.

I have something better.

When I was a child I went on a long train trip with my mom and my three sisters. We traveled from a tiny prairie town toward a strange mysterious city called Ottawa. But I knew it would be okay because I was with them and they loved me.

The older I get, the more I'm convinced that dying will be like that. And even though I've done some utterly stupid and even a few downright wicked things, it's going to be okay.

And that is enough.

Seeing Tigers

There's a cute Esso commercial playing in our area. Cute but sad.

We hear a child saying, "Grandpa, you always come to Esso, don't you?"

"Been coming here for years," says Grandpa.

"Bet I know why," says the boy.

Grandpa should have asked for the child's opinion, but instead babbles on about friendly service and that sort of pap.

"But did you ever see a tiger?" The boy wants to get back to the real issue. The picture shows us a cartoon figure of a tiger smiling at the boy through the window.

"Oh, I'm too old to see tigers," says Grandpa, very kindly. "Do you see tigers?"

The boy then does what any small Grandpa-admiring boy would do. "I'm too old to see tigers," he says, even as he tenderly, and sadly, touches the hand of the tiger against the glass of the car window. The boy knows that if he is to become a man like his grandpa, the tiger must go.

As commercials go, it is certainly one of the least offensive, and there is a tenderness to it that is refreshing.

The truth is that grandpa and Esso really *can't* see tigers. Small boys can, but old boys like grandpas and big corporations soon convince them that imaginary tigers don't exist. So small boys stop seeing them.

I feel sad every time I see that commercial.

I feel sad because children are taught not to value or believe the richness of their own God-given imagination. The hard-nosed, no nonsense, business-is-business attitude we instill in our children robs them of a way of seeing – robs them of the ability to see beyond the obvious, beyond the measurable, into the mind of God. And our children grow up spiritually handicapped.

It's not a modern phenomenon. Jesus encountered tiger-denying grandfathers and oil company advertising people too. He called them scribes and Pharisees. So Jesus picked up a child and said, "Unless you become like this child – this child who knows about imaginary tigers – all you will see is just another gas station, and you will never know the truth that lies beyond the facts."

So Jesus gathered some friends, men and women who had not lost their childhood eyes, so that when they faced the hard fact of his execution, when they faced a love-denying world, they would remember him saying to them, "You will see tigers!"

We Clapped Our Hands for the Comet

Nobody organized it. I don't remember hearing it from anyone. But we got up at three in the morning. We took a large thermos full of thick, hot, *chokolade* as we walked quietly to the beach. We knew most of our village would be there as well.

The year was 1965. We lived in the little city of Dumaguete, in the central Philippines. Two amateur Japanese astronomers, Ikeya and Seki, had discovered the new spectacular, sun-grazing comet. We soon learned it could be seen rising from the ocean just before dawn.

It was dark, as only a moonless tropical night can be dark. Our slippered feet seemed to have a strange awareness of the familiar road we couldn't see. Our eyes were on the soft black outline of coconut palms near the beach.

We walked without speaking. I held Bev's hand and four-year-old Kari clutched mine. Brave Mark, now almost six, walked very close to Bev carrying the *chokolade*.

"Dad! Look at the stars!" he whispered.

I had been trying to see the black road. I hadn't noticed.

"Yes, look at them, my son," I thought to myself. "Look at them with all the wonder of your almost-six-year-old eyes, because you will never see them this way again." I felt Kari's cheek against my hand.

The quiet coolness of the sea brushed our faces as we neared the beach and the soft smell of coral sea. Tiny reflections of stars sparkled on the gentle swell as it lapped the sand, blending its rhythm with the musical Cebuano spoken by tiny groups of people we couldn't see in the darkness.

Then, from a few yards down the beach, a muted exclamation. "Sus!" A soft halo of blue-orange light had begun to trace the edge of Sikijor Island hulking on the horizon. Almost imperceptibly the halo grew, till now it was a soft-edged fan, painted with quiet watercolor strokes upward from the island. Tiny stars sparkled through the colors, suddenly so far away, the universe given dimension by the broad tail of a comet close to earth.

I knew, or thought I knew, what comets looked like. I remembered from my childhood, inch-long pictures in a book.

But this comet rose, tail first, spreading its pale fire up and up. Soon it pained our necks to see the top straight up above our heads, a huge, half-open fan. We couldn't see it all at once, but swept our eyes up and down the gentle, orange-blue fire, so soft in places, we wished the stars would dim so we could see the fragile colors.

Far out on the sea, the shout of fisherfolk announced the first catch of the morning.

The first streaks of dawn encroached upon our comet. As if to win the race with sunlight, the bright, pale-golden coma freed itself suddenly from behind the silhouette of Sikijor Island, then stretched its paleness from horizon to the brightening black of sky above us.

And we, tiny humans gathered on that beach, applauded. We clapped our hands for our comet to hear – clapped and cheered, and then fell silent as it faded from sight before the morning sun.

For several moments we sat there, a hundred people from a tiny village, looking to each other's eyes to see reflected there our miracle. The Southern Cross flickered its benediction as it too faded in the sun.

Then someone, in a soft Cebuano said the ancient words:

When I look at your heavens,
the work of your fingers,
the moon and the stars that you have ordained,
who are we that you think of us –
fragile humans – that you care for us?*

And wordless, we all walked home.

* from Psalm 8

Gifts and Miracles

It was a gift.

Bev and I had no idea there would be a major and complete solar eclipse – the sun would be hidden by the moon – except for a spectacular corona the like of which would not be seen this way for many lifetimes. We had come to Encinedas on the California coast because we found an inexpensive motel there. And we thought perhaps it might be sunny.

We heard of the eclipse by accident, and so found ourselves on the beach with thousands of others, curious and eager.

As we stood and waited, I felt a gentle arm around my knee and glanced down to see a small boy of five or six, to whom one blue-jeaned leg was much like any other. His head leaned easily against my hip, and just as easily and naturally my hand went down to rest upon his shoulder.

"Don't look up, little boy," I thought. "Don't look up because then you will know I am not your father, and you will be embarrassed. You will not know the tender moment you have given me. You will not know the soft memories you have brought to mind, of days when I was a young father with children your age who would come and hold my leg and lean their trusting heads against me and my hand could rest on their young shoulders just as my hand rests on your young shoulder now."

The boy's mother broke the magic, as a mother must. "Kevin, that's not your dad."

I was glad she said it gently. The boy looked up and moved away and I said "Thank you. That was a kind thing you did for me." The boy had no words, just large eyes from the safe haven of his mother, but she smiled kindly and I knew she understood the moment as a touch of grace.

Then the huge magnificence took shape before us, the moon that moved in slow and measured increments to hide the flaming sun – moved until it hid the light and left us only the eternal outer circle of the sun.

And then the moon and sun together dipped into the sea and people clapped and danced their wordless prayer of thanks and we went home.

And I was thankful for a small child's tenderness and for the majesty of moon and sun in confluence, not knowing which of those to call the greater gift or miracle.

A Walking Miracle

Mel Laine lay in a ditch, almost every bone in his chest and his skull crushed by a hit-and-run driver.

In the Edmonton hospital, they told his mother that Mel had only a few hours to live.

But Mel didn't die. He hung on to life. But then his doctors had even more devastating news. Mel would spend the rest of his life comatose. A vegetable.

That was 10 years before Mel walked into a friend's living room, shook my hand, and then over many cups of coffee told me his story.

It's a long story. A story of miracles, but not the kind you see on TV. Miracles that took days and weeks and years of slow, painful loving.

It began with the long and active vigil of his mother and a special friend who believed that Mel was still there, an individual inside that living corpse on the hospital bed. The miracle grew with the encouragement of several doctors who honored their faith. It was sustained by the community of Woodcliff United Church in Calgary. Working in shifts, they talked to Mel, believing he could understand. They massaged and manipulated the muscles in his limp body. Volunteers from the church put Mel through every exercise they could imagine.

It took ten years. But I saw the miracle walk and talk and tell me about the employment training he was scheduled to undertake.

There was more to the miracle than Mel. The Woodcliff Church set up a society to work with others that the medical profession had given up on. The "walking dead" some call them. And the miracles continue. None as spectacular as Mel's, but every bit as real.

How do Mel's mom and her friends do it? "We have a lot of laughs," she says. "And a hot line to God when we start feeling discouraged."

Mother's Strong Arms

Mother had aged ten years in 12 months. It's not that there was anything wrong, it's just that everything was wrong.

The fingers that could crochet a pair of slippers in half an hour simply wouldn't move anymore.

The heart that had laughed and cried with all the many people she loved, had developed a malfunction. That never stopped her heart from loving, but last Saturday it stopped her heart from beating.

Mother knew death was near. But she wasn't afraid of death. It was the dying that was so painful, so frightening.

Mother and I had a long talk in the hospital a few months ago. She held my hand very tightly and asked, "You won't abandon me just because I'm so useless?"

"Of course not, Mom. How could I abandon you?"

"But I'm so useless. I can't do anything anymore. I'm not good for anything."

"Mom, I love you. Of course I won't abandon you. Neither will the rest of your family."

"But what good am I? I can't do anything except just sit here and stare at the walls." At first I thought Mother's fear was of being abandoned by her children. But that wasn't it. She knew us better than that.

Her pain was far deeper. It was the pain our whole society inflicts on us – that teaches us we are valued for what we can produce, by how well we can perform, by what we can achieve. It was a pain we all share.

Of course, deep down Mother knew the greater truth. Earlier we had been talking about the latest great-grandchild. He had been born on Valentine's day, and we laughed over a photograph showing a heart-shaped birthmark on his bottom.

"I guess babies can't do anything either," she said.

I knew what she meant. Babies are useless, but they are precious. Old people are useless, but they are precious.

In fact all of us, when you come right down to it, are pretty useless. But we are precious. Precious I hope, to other people. Precious at least to God, who sees the sparrow fall and numbers the hairs on our head.

"Mom," I said. "Do you remember how often you told me about the time when I was just a kid, and I'd be playing out in the back yard, and every once in a while I would run into the house and I would leap up into your arms and get a quick hug, and then run right back out again?"

She held my hand a little tighter. She remembered.

"Mom, you had strong arms, and even though I'd take a flying leap at you, you'd always catch me and give me a hug."

She smiled. "I couldn't catch you in my arms anymore, Ralph."

"I know Mom. But I still come running in for a hug. Only now, you catch me with your heart."

East of Eden

I am a most joyful man. Full of joy.

Because Zoë Rachel was born three days ago. And she (like every child) is a most wonderful and beauteous creation.

She has not replaced her brother Jake as theologian in my life. She has joined him. And her first lesson to me came three hours after she was born, as I held her there in the hospital room, Mom and Dad and Grandma beaming beside me, young Jake deciding that the hospital equipment was actually more interesting than this tiny stranger.

Zoë yawned and grimaced and frowned a little. She was thinking. That tiny head, three hours into the world, was thinking!

But how can such a newborn think? What does she know? She has no words. We've not yet seen the color of her eyes. But something is happening in that tiny mind to cause a grimace and a frown. What kind of consciousness is there in this infant that I already love so much?

I hand Zoë to her grandma who is grinning for her turn, and go to rescue Jacob from the mysterious paraphernalia of hospitals. He grins and stretches out the hands that say, "Pick me up." Jake has words now. Well, only two or three quasi words. But his face is most expressive and his body language tells us what he needs. He certainly can think. But what?

I think I think in words, but Jake quite clearly thinks far more than the two or three words he pronounces. What secret knowledge does this grandchild have? What could he teach his granddad?

God tickles us with such imponderables, and then teases us with other mysteries. Are we created just to ask such questions?

Questions such as, "Why is there pain and awfulness? Why wasn't Zoë born into a world of peace and beauty and tranquillity? Why must we all grow old and die?

Zoë probably is wiser than us all. She simply sleeps and eats and lives in all the grace that newborns know. Zoë lives in Eden – in the garden of her innocence, where love, not knowledge, is her first reality.

Jake is glancing down the pathway to the gate. Just the other day he pushed at a lamp. His mother asked him not to, for the lamp might fall. Jake didn't move, so mother picked him up and placed him firmly somewhere else. Jake walked back to the lamp and touched it, all the while studying his mom to see what she might do. Jake is reaching for the fruit of Eden – his necessary toddler steps away from innocence.

I left Eden so very long ago. Innocence is now a faded memory – a vague sense of what I've lost and where I must, someday, return. Death closes all, and beyond that only hope.

But first I'll live the Sabbath of my life, and there I know that I must listen well to Zoë and to Jake. I've heard the ancient words, "Unless you become a child, you cannot go into that Sabbath, to that time of peace and joy and hope."

To Make the World Beautiful

We're watching the salmon in their spectacular spawning run up the Adams River in British Columbia. Thousands of them, millions more likely, struggle up the river of their birth to lay their eggs and die. Their corpses litter the banks of the water, but their decomposing bodies feed microscopic organisms, which feed larger organisms, which feed small marine life which feed more fish.

"The circle of life," as the Disney film *Lion King* describes it. The biologist at Adams River pointed out that except for humans, every life form lives within that circle. The goal of life for every bird and plant and animal and fungus is to reproduce, to pass its genes along, and (where applicable) to train the young in the skills of survival, then to die. "Once you've done that," said the biologist, "if you're still around, you are just taking up space. Only humans violate that law of nature, which is not the survival of the individual but the survival of the species."

I squirm over that all the way home. I've had my children. They are all adults. So according to that biologist, I am just taking up space. I am violating the law of nature, or at least the Walt Disney theology, and by my very presence I'm endangering the human species. The decent thing for me to do would be to die.

But just a damn minute. The law of the jungle, the law of nature, isn't the only law. If we lived by the law of nature, we'd kill the weakest of our young, we'd let the elderly starve, and only the strongest males would get to pass their genes on to succeeding generations. There is another, stronger law of love and beauty and justice that defines our life.

Humans are more than intelligent animals. I come from a tradition that claims humans have something distinctly divine about them. Our lives have value, in and of themselves. My call in life is more than simply to inseminate as many females as possible. I am not a glorified baboon (some of my critics notwithstanding). I have love to share with my family and friends, I have ideas to express. I can participate and make a contribution in the social, political and spiritual life of my community.

Or is that all just pious cant? Is the biologist right? There are real signs that the human species may destroy itself by its profligate consumption.

A friend is suffering from Alzheimer's. When the disease was first diagnosed, she told us she intended to take her own life before the disease advanced too far. But it came sneaking up on her, and she no longer knows her own condition – no longer able to make that terrible decision to "end my life before I become a living corpse."

When do we become a living corpse? It's a terrifying question that isn't helped by the measurement of brain waves. Brain waves and heart beats only tell us if the organism is functioning.

Humans are more than brains and hearts, and our lives may end long before the organism quits.

On a cruise ship to Alaska, we take a side trip at one of the ports and watch the salmon spawn, and I remember Adams River and the biologist. I remember him again while I sit in a lounge aboard the ship making small-talk with a couple from Los Angeles. Both of them were slightly drunk, and told me more about themselves than they knew. *In vino veritas.* They obviously didn't like each other very well. It was a relationship of convenience because neither of them had other options. No children. No relatives or friends they cared about. All they had was money, and they were trying hard to spend it "so the government wouldn't get its hands on it." The only way they could tolerate existence was to marinate their brains in booze.

Were they alive?

The next morning, the cruise ship stops at the foot of Hubbard glacier. Miles of grandeur as the morning mists open up before us – deep blue and opal ice, hundreds of years old, slowly shifting down the slopes into the fjord. Hundreds of us lean over the rail, drinking in the majesty. The glacier "calves," an iceberg the size of many houses, crashing, thundering into the fjord. We gasp. There is awe on many faces.

I notice something else. Almost all the heads are gray. The majority of my fellow passengers are older than I – retired folks. And it occurs to me that their vocation at this moment is to stand in awe of this magnificence.

Remember the old philosophical puzzle? "If a tree falls in the forest and there is no one there to hear it, does it make a sound?"

If a glacier shines in the wilderness and there is no one there to gasp at its glory, is it beautiful? If "beauty is in the eye of the beholder" as the old philosopher said, then that glacier was not beautiful until the morning we beheld it.

Maybe that's our calling, our vocation, those of us with gray heads standing there at that ship's railing, to simply stand in awe of this creation and thus to make it beautiful. Maybe humans have a larger purpose than to simply spawn, to pass on our genes and know-how, then to die.

Perhaps that's it. Perhaps that's what we're called to be – the audience before which God's creation is revealed and made magnificent. Perhaps the calling of the old is to point with joy at all creation – glaciers, children, wrinkled hands, spawning salmon, old lace, memories and music – to notice all the preciousness and thus make God's creation beautiful and good.

That may not be much.

But on the other hand, maybe that is everything!

Unlikely Angels

Our tour bus had stalled in the wilderness, somewhere in the Negev desert. I was with a group of 30 Roman Catholic priests on a study tour of Israel. We had climbed the Moses mountain, listened to the bearded monks at their ramshackle monastery, and wondered at the mystery that brings tourists and pilgrims by the thousands to this god-forsaken place where Moses heard the voice of God.

The unforgiving sun had scorched the sand and rocks until they were too hot to touch. As far as I could see – nothing but flat desert rubble. No traffic on the road in either direction. Our group huddled in the narrow shade of our stranded bus. The tour director became elaborately cheerful and tried, without success, to organize some silly games.

I was afraid. This was serious.

Someone ventured a bit of black humor about composing the note that would be found in his shriveled hand when our desiccated bodies were discovered ten years later. Somebody else remembered Jesus' wilderness experience. And someone mentioned Moses. "Now I know how they must have felt."

"You either get religious in a place like this or you go crazy."

Then along the dusty road came a taxi. Yes, a cab, out there in the middle of nowhere, and it was available. The tour director hopped in, and without even a wave, did a U-turn and disappeared over the horizon in a cloud of dust. We assumed he was going for help, but somehow it looked more like an escape.

Again, the gloom and the anxiety settled over the hot and frightened group. We waited. And we waited. Beside me, someone began to pray quietly.

Then, from the other direction, another vehicle. We rubbed our eyes. Were we hallucinating? Were we dreaming a scene from Monty Python? Coming toward us was – yes it was – an ice-cream truck! This mirage was big and white and had ice-cream treats painted on it.

But it didn't have ice cream. It had something even better – a large tank of ice-water, and my that water was sweet and cold and wonderful. Not only that, the driver knew how to fix our bus and soon our creaky vehicle was puffing and snorting down the road again. No one wondered any longer where our tour director was.

The angels ministered to Jesus and to Moses and to us in that same wilderness. Our angel drove an ice-cream truck.

As our bus coughed its way down that desert road, I heard again the call of a desert God who sends us angels in our wilderness – unlikely angels with cool water for our thirsting, fearful souls – angels who understand and help us with our brokenness.

This caring God calls us to become unlikely angels too, offering cold water and a helping hand to frightened travelers – to share the gifts we have been given.

And this desert deity smiles and chuckles when an Arab ice-cream driver teaches priests and writers about God.

Suspended Disbelief

There are moments.

Moments when, just for an instant, you know. There is certainty and a sense of call. Those moments are rare because such a sense of purpose can so easily lead to arrogance. Or madness.

He was a young, heavily bearded Russian Orthodox monk, who spoke a cultured Oxford English. "Please remove your shoes," he asked politely.

St. Catherine's Monastery is in the desert of Sinai, undoubtedly the bleakest piece of real estate on God's earth. It is at the foot of "Mt. Moses," or "Jebel Musa" or "Mt. Sinai."

"It is on this mountain that Moses received the Ten Commandments," the bearded monk had told us.

Was this really the place? Did Moses really go up a mountain? Was there such a person as Moses, or is he simply a legendary figure to whom, in the course of time, many other legends from various tribes and nations were ascribed?

Look at the path leading up that mountain. Those stones are worn smooth – worn smooth by the thousands and thousands of pilgrims who have come here from every corner of the globe to remember. To remember God's great gift of the law. God's great gift of presence. And God's call to unqualified and unprepared people to go and struggle for freedom.

There may not have been a historical Moses, and this may not be the mountain, but pilgrims from around the world have polished those stones with their faith and made this mountain a holy place. Whatever else it is, it is a good place to reflect on God's encounter with humanity – on God's call to humanity.

Down, deep inside the monastery, we took off our shoes and moved silently into a small, sparse, unadorned room. "This is the place," whispered the monk, "where Moses met God in the burning bush. Let us be silent for awhile, and remember."

I had a choice. I've done a lot of reading, study, research and I probably knew as much as that bearded Monk about Moses and the legends that surround him. My cynical intellect was working overtime. But then a concept came to me from my work in theater. "Suspended disbelief." If I could suspend my disbelief for just a while, I might enter into that moment. I could experience the spirit or analyze the history. But not both.

The cool sand on the floor soothed my tired feet as I sat on a rock and made my choice. We sat in silence, thinking, meditating, reflecting, soaking up the holiness that filled the room.

And in the silence, in that moment came an instant of absolute certainty. God reaches out to frightened shepherds like Moses and frightened writers like Ralph and gives the gift of holiness and insight. And a sense of being called.

"Go down, Moses, Ralph. Tell those pharaohs back in Canada. Let my people go."

Right Brain, Left Brain

Have you been keeping up with scientific research lately? I have. I read all the major scholarly journals, like *Reader's Digest*, *TV Guide*, and *Redbook*.

One of the things the scientists have been fussing over lately is the connection between the mind and the body. Turns out you can't tell where one begins and the other leaves off. They are both part of the same thing called "human." Now you and I could have told them that, but scientists have to prove everything before they can believe anything.

I don't play the piano, so I wouldn't know, but apparently there is something like a "memory" in the fingers that retains certain combinations of musical notes. That's true on my computer, for sure, because my fingers have memorized a bunch of key strokes that misspell the same words over and over again.

For instance, I belong to the United Church but I keep typing it "Untied Chruch." We used to call that a Freudian slip, but now I can blame it on my fingers which have a mind of their own and are only sometimes connected to my brain.

A friend who counsels folk who have been abused as children tells me that in the process of therapy, when they are trying to remember what actually happened, people sometimes feel the pain in the places where they were injured as children, and occasionally even a bruise reappears. "Memory isn't just lodged in the brain," he says, "it is lodged in the whole body."

Everything is connected to everything else. Here I am, right on the edge of retirement, and I realize that though I am in good health and my finances are pretty well in order (I won't have to live on tuna sandwiches, but neither will I feast on pheasant under glass), I may have forgotten the crucial fact that my body and my pocket book are organically connected to my mind and my soul.

I realize how many of my friends, mostly male friends, complain about health problems just at the point of retirement. I can name a half dozen men I know who died within a year of hanging up the skates.

That's the bad news. The good news is that an equal number seem to have blossomed into renewed health and vigor as they retire. The point is that one way or another, physical health is directly connected to who we think we are and what we do to justify ourselves.

There's a spiritual connection too. I'm not really sure what we mean when we talk about soul, but I'm convinced that you and I have one. I don't think it's a wisp of smoke, or a white bed-sheet that floats heavenward when we die. Maybe a soul is all those qualities of humanness that we can't explain any other way.

Those same scientists who have discovered (ta-dum!) that mind and body are connected have now discovered something else most humans have known since Moses was a pup. The mind, body and *spirit* are all connected. The folks at the "Y" used to have it in their symbol (remember the "mind-body-spirit" triangle?) before they got embarrassed about their religious roots and stopped calling themselves the "Young Men's *Christian* Association." The founders of the "Y" knew. The folks who are running the "Y" now are just rediscovering the elementary fact that the human is body, mind, and something wonderfully mysterious called the spirit or soul or life force.

Books by folks like Larry Dossey, M.D. (*Healing Words, Prayer is Good Medicine*) recount scientifically precise experiments that have demonstrated beyond reasonable doubt that prayer actually does work – prayer does help people heal. Dossey has concluded that for him, as a doctor, not to pray for people would be to withhold a powerful therapy and would constitute malpractice.

The fact that prayer doesn't always work means nothing. None of the other medical prescriptions *always* work either. But now they have statistics to prove what many of us knew all along, that it helps to pray for folks who are sick, and it helps to pray for yourself when you are sick.

Don't you feel so much better now that you have statistics to prove what you knew all along?

There's probably no wisdom more ancient or more universal than the idea that humans are not cobbled together with a bit of this and a bit of that – we are one whole entity and are connected to everything. This is central to Buddhist teaching, for instance. (No, I will not tell you the awful joke about the Buddhist monk who said to the hot-dog vendor, "Make me one with everything.")

Priests and shamans and teachers of every major faith have known that since the dawn of human experience.

Body, mind, soul are all connected.

We are all connected to each other.

How about that!

Promises and Rainbows

The clear, pure light of the sun warms the whole earth, and all the people on it.

When sunlight shines through a prism, the light spreads it-self into a rainbow of colors, all the colors we humans have ever imagined. Every shade is different. But no color is better than the other.

God's light shines through all creation. As it shines through the lives and traditions of many people, we see God's light as a rainbow of expressions – Christian, Hindu, Sikh, Moslem, Jew, aboriginal traditions and many, many more. As God's light shines through the prism of the human race, it is sometimes distorted and sometimes hidden, but it always breaks through and colors our world with glory.

There's an ancient legend about Noah. We all know the part about the animals getting onto the ark. But the best part of the story is at the end. When the flood is over and the sun is shining on the earth, God commissions Noah and all his descendants (that's us) to treasure the earth and care for it. God says, in effect, "You do your part and I'll do mine, and here's a rainbow to remind us of that understanding. The covenant."

Years ago when Mark, my eldest child, was a budding young scientist, he explained prisms and water droplets and rainbows to me. "But when there's dirt in the air – smog and stuff – the light can't refract and you don't get rainbows."

If we foul our world with hatred – if we pollute our world with greed – the rainbow can't happen.

The rainbow is a symbol of God's presence in many traditions. The sunlight, shining through millions of droplets of water, each one a prism, lights up the world with color even as thunderclouds still roll on the horizon.

Laughing with God

Spirituality Is Like Sex

You've seen the painting called American Gothic? It shows the old farmer with the pitchfork standing with his wife in front of the old farm house, both of them looking as if they've just had an unanesthetized root canal. That's the face of religion for many people. It's the kind of religion your mother said was good for you, the way eating raw broccoli is good for you. The way jogging is good for you.

Have you ever seen a happy jogger?

Have you seen religious people who look like joggers, sweating and trying so hard to do the right thing, they forget to be human in the process? Some of them are so heavenly minded, they are no earthly good. They get so uptight about the things they believe, they're as much fun as a caged hyena. And I am talking about folks from all over the religious spectrum – the far-out New Age types, born-again evangelicals, stuffy traditional Protestants or Catholics, native spiritual leaders, Muslim fanatics and Buddhist basket cases.

Spirituality should be fun. In fact, spirituality is like sex. If you're not having fun, you're not doing it right.

And for most people it *is* fun. There's a strong element of fun in all the great spiritual traditions.

But unfortunately, lots of religious people look like that couple in American Gothic. There are some branches of the major religions that do a kind of spiritual lobotomy on folks and turn them into social zombies. Those pseudo-spiritual groups attract followers who enjoy wallowing in guilt, the folks who are convinced that if it's fun, it must be indecent, immoral, or fattening. All they've read in their scriptures is the phrases that begin, "Thou shalt not..."

Those phrases are in the scriptures all right, and for good reason. There are things we do that make nobody happy, like killing and cheating and lying and ripping people off. Those things are prohibited in every major religion in the world and in almost every legal system. The laws in our country are based on those. Without them, we'd have social anarchy.

But you can be a totally wonderful person and never do anything wrong and still be as uptight as a Baptist at a bacchanalia. Doing everything right is not the same as being happy.

I know the Bible better than any of the other scriptures, so I'll use that as an example.

There's no commandment anywhere in the Bible that says, "Don't have fun." There's nothing that says you need to walk around with your eyes turned up into your head looking "holy" (or slightly stoned), or that you shouldn't enjoy a lively party or a good joke. In fact, one of the words that you read over and over in the Bible is "joy!" There's far more about joy in the Bible than keeping your nose clean.

Jesus was not a standup comedian, but he had a lively, rollicking sense of humor. He knew how to have fun and he loved a party. In fact, some of his more anal contemporaries got on his case because he had a reputation for hanging around with the "wrong" people. Jesus enjoyed his friends, and he had a lot of them – hookers and winos among them. He told jokes, and he wasn't above pulling someone's leg a little. He loved kids.

Actually, Jesus was far more concerned about what people were like, than what they did or believed. A rich yuppie once asked him, "What do I have to do to get into heaven?"

"Love," said Jesus. "Love God with everything you've got. And love other people as much as you love yourself."

"That's pretty tough," said the yuppie.

"You're right," Jesus said, grinning from ear to ear. "Getting a rich yuppie into heaven is as hard as getting a camel through the eye of a needle. But, with a little help from God, it can be done."

Is that all there is to it?

Yes.

But don't be fooled. It's no easy thing. It's easy enough to love "humanity" in the abstract or the street children of Rio whom we've only read about, but it is not so easy to love the neighbor who parks his car across my driveway and allows his dog to bark all night. It's not so easy to love some of the turkeys I work with. It is especially not easy to love my own family all the time. (They always find me totally, 100 percent lovable.)

But loving people puts a lot of fun back into life. Real fun, the kind of fun you feel good about, the kind of fun that fills you up instead of emptying you out, is the kind of fun you are only going to have with people you love.

If you come out of your temple or church or synagogue look-ing as if you've been sucking on a lemon, then there's something really wrong with your spirituality. If you feel like those folks in

American Gothic look, then there is something fundamentally haywire with your life and your religious outlook.

It's like sex. Spirituality should be spontaneous and joyful and passionate.

Your spiritual life should do many things with you and for you, but one of the things it should do (if it is genuine) is help you be happier than you would be without it.

And being happy is fun.

The Little Demi-God in My Head

I read it in a scientific book. It had to be scientific and authoritative, because it had lots of footnotes and was really boring.

It's now official that mind, body and soul are all part of the same human person. Some scientist figured out a way to test that, so what all of us have known all along is officially true. We can talk about it now without embarrassment.

I hope that now the scientific types will get on to discovering a cure for a favorite problem of mine. It has something to do with the mind, body, and soul not getting their act together. It goes like this.

Why is it that halfway through the process of doing something I forget what it is that I'm doing? For instance, I will go from the bedroom to the kitchen to get something. By the time I get to the kitchen I forget what it is I went there for, and then stand there in the middle of the kitchen with a silly look on my face.

It's worse when I have to go and get a hammer or a pair of pliers from the garage to fix something in the house. The garage is just out the back door, but by the time I get there, my mind has gone on to something else and I'm standing there in the freezing cold wondering what I came for.

So I take a flying guess and come back with a screwdriver or an oil can. And Bev gives me a strange look because she knows I wanted to pull a nail.

There have been times when I was driving somewhere in the car, and it seemed to drive itself while my mind was busy arguing with something I just heard on the radio, and suddenly I wind up back home and that isn't where I intended to go at all. At least not until I had been wherever it was I was going in the first place.

My friends call it premature senility, but it's not true. I've been that way ever since I was a kid. The problem is the way my mind is organized.

Some people's minds are organized like a computer, with everything exactly where they put it.

My mind is organized like my daughter's bedroom in her teenage years. Everything she owned was there, spread evenly about six inches deep on her bedroom floor. Whenever she wanted something, she only had about a ten percent chance of finding it, but she often found something else more interesting she had forgotten about. Now that she's an adult and picks up her own stuff, life is not nearly as interesting.

A while back I read a book about how the mind is organized into the left brain and the right brain. The left side of the brain controls the right side of the body and the right brain controls the left side of the body. It took me days to work that through in my mind, so don't get upset if it sounds confusing at first. It means that only left-handed people are in their right minds.

The left brain is the manager. The left brain looks after getting your shoes tied, getting to work on time, and remembering to take out the garbage before your spouse yells at you. My left brain doesn't do that part at all well. What it does well is the talking part.

The right brain is the creative department. This is where

you do your imagining, your loving, where you experience your feelings for others. This is where you store old stories and songs.

My right brain works overtime. I can remember every joke I ever heard. No, I don't mean that I can tell a string of jokes, or that if someone tells a joke about a traveling salesperson that I can haul out 15 on the same topic. Not at all. But as soon as the joke starts, if I've heard it before, I remember it. But I laugh anyway.

And songs. I was a disc jockey in the 1950s. I remember every song that was on the hit parade at that time. No, I can't list them off for you, but if someone starts one, I'm off. I can sing the whole thing, with the exact vocal nuances. I can still do a passable imitation of Johnny Ray sobbing through *Cry* or Frankie Lane belting out *The Ghost Riders*.

Remembering old jokes and old songs may be fun, but it doesn't put jam on the toast. The world loves us right-brained folks but will never give us a job or put us in charge of anything. So out of necessity (not choice, believe me!) we go to career development seminars in expensive hotels led by earnest – no, evangelical – young executives in tailored suits who preach to us about the virtues of organization and planning.

Sitting on my desk right in front of me – it's been sitting there for a year – is a wonderful Pocket Organizer – an electronic gizmo that will keep track of my entire life, record everything I am supposed to remember and make frozen daiquiris. It comes with a manual an inch thick. So far, I have learned to turn it on.

Right-brained people generally succumb to the demands of a left-brained world that values results and statistics and columns of figures and anything you can measure. It values reliability, dependability, profitability. So we right-brained people pretend we are left-brained and try to learn to act that way. Most of us manage. Sort of.

Late at night, as we lie in bed, we have our secret fantasies of writing a poem or symphony, singing in a rock concert, painting a masterpiece. In the morning, the dream is gone so we brush our teeth, drink black coffee, and brace ourselves for the world of sales seminars and spreadsheets and left-brained leaders.

But the muse will not be muted. That little demi-god who bounces around in your head, tickling the insides of your ears, can never be totally silenced. In the middle of a planning session at the office, when the sales manager is talking about sales curves, you pick up on one syllable and in your mind you are Frankie Lane singing "Mule train...clippity cloppin' over hill and dale..." and you miss the next ten minutes of terribly important information.

Or you have your head under the sink fixing a leak, and you go to the garage for a pipe wrench, but on your way past the washing machine with the bottle of spot remover on it, you become Lady Macbeth saying "Out! Out! Damned spot!" So you come back with the oil can in your hand and your spouse gives you one of those strange, long-suffering looks.

The hardest part is when things strike you as funny when it really would be much more polite not to laugh.

Once, on an airplane, I got into a conversation with a terribly serious veterinarian from Trochu, Alberta. He was dressed very formally in a pin-striped three piece suit with a button down collar and conservative tie. He was telling me, in more detail than I really wanted, how to find out if cows are pregnant.

"You have to push your hand in up to your elbow and see if you can feel the calf," he said solemnly.

"How often do you do that?"

"I sometimes do several hundred cows a day."

It all started to strike me as very funny – the image of this neatly dressed man thrusting his arm in and out of the south end of cows.

Then I started giggling because it occurred to me that a cow which had lost its calf would be "decaffeinated." "De-calf..." Never mind.

But you see what I mean? My problem is not all that terribly serious, I suppose. And it probably won't get much attention from psychiatrists and biologists working on the connection between mind and body. They have better things to do like discovering a cure for terminal acne.

I wonder, though, if the right brain is connected directly to the soul. Us right-brained folks have been soul brothers and sisters for generations, hearing the soul music, seeing the soul in each other even as we muddle through the chaos of our lives. We have laughed and cried at the wonder of it all, but sometimes felt very handicapped in this left-brained computer organized world.

I'm grateful that the left-brained scientific types have discovered soul with their statistics. I just hope they know that a soul is a living thing – that if you cut it up into pieces to examine it, you'll kill it.

That's the thing about soul.

It's got to be touched and loved.

Or it dies.

And if the soul dies, so does everything else.

Toilet Training Tourists

What travel agents never tell you is that North American tourists going to Europe need to be housebroken. Mostly that involves learning the one critical life skill – to laugh at yourself. Without that, the Belgians can reduce you to a bowl of emotional jelly in a week. The Italians can do it in a day.

European culture has great variety – fine wines, great music, and incomprehensible toilets. American civilization has only two kinds of wine (red and white) and two kinds of music (country and old-time fiddlers). There isn't much variety in toilets either.

Europeans want the necessities of life to be interesting. North Americans want them to be functional. Europeans in charge of getting stuff in and out of human bodies are mad, slightly drunk artists from the left bank of the Seine. North Americans in charge of the ingress and egress of food and drink are nerdy types with computers.

The travel agents know about all this, but they keep it a secret, and recruit unsuspecting folks with "leadership qualities" to be Tour Group Leaders. Someone has to guide these naïve North Americans, who want their food pronounceable and their toilets flushable, into a world where food must have *élan* and the toilets must offer a challenge. Successful Tour Group Leaders combine the skills of sheep dog, den mother and priest, but above all a mentor in the fine art of life. Tour Group Leaders must keep the group laughing – preferably at themselves.

We led a gaggle of 39 tourists around Europe on one of those "if this is Tuesday, it must be Belgium" kind of junkets. "Led" is an overstatement. Bev walked at the head of the pack throwing body blocks and temper tantrums, tripping, doing whatever was necessary to slow them down. I ran back and forth across the back of the herd like a Scottish sheep dog, nipping at heels, barking at the laggards, and generally making myself the most unpopular person in the group.

The food was not too much of a problem because tour busses only stop at places where the waiters have North Americans psyched and give them a steak sandwich and coffee or a hamburger and coke regardless of what they may order. As long as we could keep them away from small restaurants up dark alleys where the waiters have black mustaches and dirty aprons, our 39 tourists did just fine on food.

But the toilets! Europeans regard toilets as an art form, not a utility. Theater art primarily, because what could be better comedy than North Americans trying to cope with European plumbing? Until we got the point of it all, we found ourselves the butt of the joke. Toilet training tourists is a matter of attitude, not technology.

One of the funniest scenes is watching a tourist try to get into a European toilet. You need a coin. So you stand in line for 45 minutes to change your money from dollars into whatever, then as you desperately fumble to find the right coin to put into the slot, you discover you have every other coin except the specific one required. So you give up and quietly wet your pants.

It was the women on our tour bus who worked out a strategy. Whenever the bus stopped in a new country, which seemed to be every hour or so, they would charge to the biffy *en mass* and line up, having sent a delegate (preferably a young husband with a good bladder) to the place where they change money. "Get one sample of every coin minted in the last 50 years!"

One of those coins would fit the slot. Once one woman got into the cubicle, she would hold the door open for the next one. And so on, so that in effect the whole bunch could go "do-do on one dime." Was that ripping off the folks who owned the bathrooms? Probably, but in a contest between distended bladders and ethics, bladders win every time. And the women learned to do it with such triumphant whoops and so much laughter, even the Germans offered a grudging admiration.

The more progressive countries posted guards in each bathroom to whom you paid your florin or francs or rasbucknicks. All the guards in the women's bathrooms were men and vice versa. Speculation on the bus had it that since the job didn't pay much, there needed to be fringe benefits. If the main reason for European toilets is to entertain Europeans, then what better way to do it than with a bit of good-natured voyeurism?

We almost lost one of our men, a retired, hypertensive banker, to this system. It was in Italy where the toilets presented even more of a challenge than in France. He came staggering back to the bus, his face beet red – hyperventilating – not seeing anything even slightly funny about anything.

"That's supposed to be the men's can, right? There's this big fat babe in there, right in the men's john, and she wants, I don't know, 10,000 lira, or something, so I give her all my money and she gives me four tiny little sheets of brown paper. Then she stands right outside the cubicle. Right outside it! I couldn't do a damn thing!"

Half an hour later, after we brought him down from the edge of an aneurysm, I visited that same facility. The staff, all women, were still laughing.

Bev also "enjoyed" an exciting toilet adventure in a busy *piazza* in Rome. Asking the question most tourists ask most often, she was directed to a stainless steel bunker right in the center of a traffic circle around a small park.

It didn't seem to have a door, but it had coin slots and a sign which asked (in four languages) for 8 million lira (about 25 cents). She dropped in the money and *voilà!* A stainless steel door slid open silently and revealed the sparkling clean facilities within.

The call of nature being stronger than her sense of foreboding, Bev went in. Silently, the door slid shut. I stood outside and wondered if I would ever see my beloved again.

Inside, Bev discovered that once the call of nature had been answered, her anxiety took over. There was no handle on the door. No button to press – no lever to pull. There was no window to wave out of. No phone to call on. No sign in any language which indicated what to do once you were done.

There was only one tiny lever. It said "Flush." In seven languages. Since she couldn't think of anything else to do, she flushed. Silently the door slid open. Sobbing our joy and relief, we rushed into each other's arms.

As we walked away, we saw a bench on which were perched four elderly men. It was situated exactly where they would get the best view when that door slid open. All the other benches in the *piazza* were empty.

"You know," said Bev, "I usually flush before I do myself up. That must be the best show in town." Then she managed a laugh and so did I.

The old men were laughing too, this time *with* us rather than *at* us. The toilets had done their job, for the Italian men and this Canadian couple. All of us learned a little of the art of life.

Who says Europeans only tolerate North Americans because of their money?

The Burnished Belly-Button Syndrome

I suffer from a terrible affliction. It's not all that rare, and the cure is well known. But that doesn't make it any easier to live with.

The technical term for my ailment is "jelly belly."

If you don't catch "jelly belly" in its earlier stages, it degenerates into something worse. A hernia. It's men who get the normal kind of hernia most often – when your insides try to get outside.

It's a difficult and sensitive issue, this thing about a hernia. It usually needs medical attention but don't go to my family doctor. See if you can find an overweight doctor with high blood pressure who understands things like herniae. My doctor is not only young and fit, but has a strong interest in sports medicine.

He goes climbing in the Himalayas!

As a result, he simply cannot understand people with my malady and insists on prescribing outrageous and unrealistic remedies.

Like exercise.

I like to get my exercise watching football on TV. He insists on things like walking or running or those social and moral abominations known as "keep-fit" classes.

The doctor prescribed the same thing for Bev – a devious and unethical strategy!

What could I do? I was outflanked and outnumbered. Off with Bev to keep-fit classes. Twice a week!

We gathered in this huge gymnasium – flabby bodies, ravaged by floods of overindulgence and sloth. What an odd assortment we were, bulging and billowing through our clothing like Michelin men in sweatsuits. There wasn't a happy face in the crowd.

"Okaaay...let's have fuuuunnnn!" calls our fitness instructor, a young woman so thin she probably only has only one stripe on her pajamas. And the music starts. It's what my daughter calls "soft rock" but it sounds not a bit soft to me. I can understand not a single word of what our instructor is yelling, but I try the best I can to imitate the pretzel twists and contortions she seems to enjoy so much.

In between pieces of music she yells, "Smile! You're having fun!"

"You may be having fun, lady," I mutter to myself, "but in the list of the 100 things I consider the most funnest, this ranks 250th."

Then we start the aerobics. That's the part where you puff and pant and get flushed in the face – the part which people my tender age should be careful with. Two-thirds of the way through we stop to take our pulse to see whether we're about to expire. I can't find my pulse, so I assume I've died and gone to hell.

By the end of the class, I'm feeling very unfit and suffering from an even worse affliction, brought on by the friction between wet sweatsuit and whatever part of your anatomy sticks out far-thest. It's known as the 3-B Syndrome (Burnished Belly Button). Bev got the same thing, only twice as bad and higher up.

What amazes me most about all this is that we started those keep-fit classes a year ago and Bev and I are still going. Twice a week. Voluntarily.

I suppose it's because I'm finding exercise increasingly nec-essary. Having been basically healthy all my life, I'd forgotten there was a body somewhere below my head that needed a little attention now and again.

The Bible speaks of the body as the "temple of the soul." My temple has started to show a fair bit of weathering here and there. Some of the roofing has blown away and the foundation is sagging. I realize now that if I'd done a bit more preventive maintenance a few years ago I wouldn't be having problems now with dry rot.

The truth is, I'm physically lazy.

I've often fantasized about what it would be like to have some nice acceptable ailment that would keep me laid up for a week so I could read and watch hockey games on TV and have a wonderful, relaxing time. Something just serious enough so I wouldn't feel guilty about goofing off, but not so serious as to really bother me.

Don, a friend of mine, broke his arm falling out of a tree. He enjoyed every minute of it. He even managed to skip work for awhile. When he went back, they assigned a flunky to drive his car, write his orders, and scratch his back. It was a great deal.

Last time I saw Don, he was back up a tree trying to fall off.

"So," I thought to myself as I sat in the doctor's office, "maybe I get to have a broken arm. Like Don."

"You have a hernia," said the doctor.

"A hernia? I was counting on a broken arm."

I had a hernia.

Hernias are in that class of ailment which humans have because we've never completely adapted to walking upright. Like varicose veins and hemorrhoids. They afflict people with flabby stomach muscles. Jelly belly.

The doctor prescribed a "hernia repair." It's a rip-off. You get one of those "in-by-nine, out-by-five" hospital routines. Nobody even has a chance to send you flowers.

Or chocolates.

I didn't even get a chance to read a magazine, much less a book. And the only reason I got a visit from my minister is because at that time my minister was Bev and she had to come drive me home.

Hernias are a signal. They say, "take care of the old bod."

My doctor tells me not to lift heavy stuff. He also tells me to stop thinking I'm somehow responsible for everything and everybody. Like my grown-up kids. Or the "world situation."

"Do the things you can do about justice and the health of your community, but don't be so conceited. It's not all up to you." The doctor's comments got me wondering if there were such things as emotional and spiritual hernias.

There must be. Jesus offered a prescription. "Consider the lilies...they goof off occasionally but God looks after them. Keep your head focused on what's really at the top of the priority list. Don't lie awake at night stewing about things you can't fix. Don't fuss about tomorrow. Tomorrow will happen whether you're there to help it or not. Focus on God's priority list and you'll be just fine." (Yeah, I know that isn't exactly the way you'd find it in the Bible. It's my own personal "translation.")

"And," said my athletic doctor, "if you invest half an hour in exercise every day, you'll probably never have another hernia."

He didn't specify which kind of exercise. Or which kind of hernia.

When God Laughs

The church bulletin announced a violin solo by Mr. Peabody.

"Friends," said the minister, "Mr. Playbody will now pee for you."

God, I am convinced, giggled along with everyone else that morning.

Well, okay, if you must have God being more dignified, then call it a "chortle" or a "chuckle," though I have no trouble with the concept of God in the third row, head back, mouth open, in a rib-shaking, eye-watering belly laugh. I'm even prepared to argue that laughter and prayer are very closely related. Occasionally they are the same thing.

That concept had me editing a newsletter called *Rumors* for ten years. In that journal, various writers pondered the connections between spirituality and humor, and I included all the religious humor I could get my hands on. *Rumors* died for some very good reasons, but here are a few *bons mots*.

There are a few chronic (perhaps Freudian) typing errors that church secretaries make. Dropping the "g" from sing happens a lot, so errors like, "The choir will sin for you," are legion. There was the typist who wrote the 6th Commandment as "Thou shalt not admit adultery" which was in the grand tradition established by the original King James Bible way back in Shakespeare's day. Probably the most valuable antique book around is called "the adulterer's Bible" because they left out one little word. It reads, "Thou shalt commit adultery."

Most clergy have learned never to dictate stuff on the phone, because the possibilities for holy confusion are wonderful. The anthem in one church bulletin was shown as, "I'll call and let you know," and in another church, "They haven't told me yet." There is a famous anthem called, *Olivet to Calvary* which appeared as "All of it to Calgary."

The very best one, as far as I know, was told to me by musician Alan Whitmore who apparently found the anthem *Panis Angelicus* shown as *Penis Angelicus*.

It gets even more dicey when you're talking to the press. The famed preacher, Ernest Marshall Howse was quoting Jesus but the reporter wrote: "Greater love hath no man than this, that he lay down his wife for his friend." And how about, "Remember in prayer the many who are sick of our church and community." Or, "For those of you who have children and don't know it, we have a nursery downstairs."

"Religious humor" was an oxymoron for me until, as a young reporter, I was assigned to a church conference to cover some very important person (whose name I have long forgotten) who was making a most important speech (on a subject I have also forgotten). What I do remember is that the speaker offered one-liners by the dozen and stories that had me literally weeping, they were so funny. Then, when the laughter reached a crescendo, he said, "Friends, if you can laugh, you can pray. Let us pray!"

The life-changing insight, that laughter and spirituality are part of the same fabric, would be called a "born again" experience by folks on the religious right, and a "paradigm shift" by those on the far left. I dislike both terms equally, but the radical truth of that man's statement made a huge difference in my life. God with a sense of humor. What a concept!

A God like that would enjoy being a judge at a religious T-shirt contest. I have my own favorites, which I think God would like. One of them, worn by my friend Patricia Baker, had elaborately filigreed lettering you had to get indecently close to read. It said, "The Ladies' Sewing Circle and Terrorist Society." And the one I saw on another preacher at a conference on prayer which read "Lettuce spray!" In an airport on a teenager: "Jesus is coming. Look busy!"

God would especially like the ones worn by a bunch of Lutherans who met in Banff to consider the ponderings of a guru who talked about a "paradigm shift" in our society. Some delegates wore T-shirts that read, "Shift happens!" and others "Holy Shift!"

A God up there in the clouds zapping sinners with thunderbolts doesn't do much for me, but a God who is down here beside us, crying and worrying and sometimes breaking out in great peals of unrestrained laughter – that kind of God I can love.

Now That's Class

There are two con artists in the jails of California who should at least get some kind of credit for having a class act.

They almost did it to Donald Richard McTavish, who not only has a double-barreled first name but a degree from Princeton and a Ph.D. in Scottish History from the University of Edinburgh. He's minister of one of those mega churches in California. Presbyterian.

It was Christmas Sunday morning. McTavish was at "thirdly" in his sermon. The congregation was quite wrapped up in the mastery of his language, the faint "burr" in his mid-western accent, his mastery of Scottish history. Only a few bothered to wonder what the sermon had to do with life in urban California.

Into the back of the church came two men dressed as Santas – red hat, black boots, the works.

Without batting an eye, they began to take up a collection.

McTavish, of course, was stunned. Had he forgotten something? Was this some special project that had slipped his mind? Was the Finance Committee unusually creative?

McTavish stood there, not knowing what to do. Or should he do anything?

Speaking softly and with practiced ease, the two Santas passed the plate down one pew after another. The dollar bills mounted up. A few people giggled. Gamely, McTavish soldiered on. "And fourrrthly..." he intoned.

Just then, a burly usher came and escorted the two Santas out into the waiting arms of a police constable. It seems the Santas had managed to successfully hit every church in the area. Like most con artists, they were done in by their own greed, and pulled their clever hoax just once too often.

There's probably a moral in that story somewhere, though I suspect I told it because I find creative crooks and shysters quite intriguing. In personality and style, they're not much different than writers. Or some clergy for that matter.

We're close enough in temperament that we can spot a class act when we see one. And the good Presbyterians in that church will remember the Santas long after McTavish and his sermon are dead and gone.

Dangerous Goods

The whole thing got blown to smithereens.

And a good thing too, because it contained dangerous goods. Subversive stuff. Explosive materials.

The folks in the neighborhood around Erskine Presbyterian Church in Hamilton, Ontario called the bomb squad. There was a mysterious package on the front steps of the church, and it had been sitting there for 12 hours. It didn't seem to have any identifying marks. No telling what it contained. No wonder the neighbors got twitchy and called the cops. They were good neighbors and they did the right thing.

The bomb squad tried to X-ray the ominous looking bundle, but that didn't work. Only one thing to do. Bring in the bazookas and blow the thing up.

Bam!

When the last piece of paper floated to the ground, they discovered what it was. Curriculum. Church school curriculum called *The Whole People of God* from a company called Wood Lake Books. The courier had delivered it early in the morning, dropped it label down on the steps, and left.

The bomb squad did the right thing. I know that curriculum pretty well – even had a hand in publishing it – and blowing it sky high is the only proper way to dispose of it. It is full of subversive ideas like "love your enemies," and "love is more important than power," and "be fair to each other, especially the folks who are at the bottom of the heap," and "it is better to give than to receive," and "justice shall flow like a river..."

Ideas like that should be blown to smithereens, because if people ever took them seriously, they would turn the world upside down.

It Never Snows Here

It was the best show in years. Vancouver in the snow is funnier than rubber toothpicks.

You notice the cars first. They go careening around in fantastic fishtails, back wheels spinning in a slow-motion ballet that ends abruptly with the crunch of fenders and tinkle of glass.

It' s not that Vancouver drivers don't know how to drive in the snow. Most of them are prairie transplants. They learned snow survival in kindergarten.

But once they move to Disneyland North, they renounce snow. It becomes an article of faith. They simply do not believe that it can snow in Vancouver. And what you believe can be a stronger reality than what you experience.

Snow tires are unofficially banned on the coast because people refuse to admit even the possibility of needing them. Neither is it cool to carry any of the paraphernalia – like snow-scrapers. The folks in Vancouver are in a desperate state of denial.

I watched a self-important junior executive in pinstripe suit, tan trench coat, and blow-dried hair scraping the ice from the windshield of his TransAm with a pocket comb. Several unsuccessful minutes later he switched to a nail file. He finally managed to make a peep hole three inches across, before he walked around to get into his car, and stepped into six inches of slush with his shiny loafers.

That got him even more annoyed, so he slammed the door, which of course brought the snow from the top of the windshield sliding over his peep hole. He jumped out, stepped in the slush again, cleaned his windshield, stepped in the slush a third time as he got back in, started the engine of his brand new, bright red TransAm, and threw it into reverse.

While he had been busy cleaning his windshield and wetting his feet, a big gray Brinks truck had parked its solid steel hulk two feet behind the TransAm.

It was not a good day for self-important junior executives.

That night I told all this to my son, who was then living there in Lotus Land. My super-intelligent son who knows everything there is to know about computers.

"But Dad." he said, "it never snows in Vancouver!"

The Worlds Oldest Joke Book

Old Don Quixote dreamed "the impossible dream" of conquering "the unbeatable foe," which included windmills. Don Quixote was not totally sane and was not voted most likely to succeed in his mission.

Bookmakers give me about the same odds. The "unreachable star" I'm stretching toward is demonstrating to everyone, from new age *aficionados* to red-eyed evangelicals that faith and fun are part of the same reality. You can't have one without the other.

"Come off it, Ralph," says the little *advocatus diaboli* (or devil's advocate – a.d. for short) in the back of my head. "Maybe, just maybe, you can make a case for real faith needing a bit of comic relief once in awhile. But everybody *knows* the devil has the best lines – that all the fun things are indecent, immoral or fattening. Fun spirituality is an oxymoron!"

Wrong. That's the problem, can't you see. We're too superficial in our understanding of spirituality. We're too superficial in our understanding of fun. We see spirituality as pie in the sky bye and bye. We see fun as escape. Vacation. Something we do when we're trying to get away from it all. Especially away from all that life requires of us. Write something funny and it is classified as "escapist" reading.

Except that in the Bible it says, "Make a joyful noise unto the Lord." You can't make a joyful noise without having fun doing it. Have you ever seen a sourpuss making a joyful noise?

It also says, "Come into God's presence with thanksgiving." Thanksgiving is fun too. At least it is for me.

"Define 'fun,'" says a.d., "because you're starting to play semantic games, and when you do that you are a crashing bore."

Okay. Fun is when you are doing something that brings you

genuine joy. You do it for the sake of doing it, not because you get airline points.

Example #1. Fun was last summer sitting under a tree on a hot summer day with Bev and my grandkids. We had two inches of water in a little plastic pool. Zoë didn't want to get wet and so played with her rattles and chewed on her toys sitting on our laps while Jake, barenaked and beautiful, splashed and giggled in the pool. Nothing was happening. And yet, in a profound way, everything was happening.

Example #2. Fun was visiting the Catacombs in Rome, listening to the care and love in the voice of the monk who showed us through those caverns, and sensing a little of the magnificent faith of our forebears who worshiped and were buried there. There were tears in my eyes as we left.

Something that seems to have escaped many gurus and sages and theologians and ecclesiastics is that humor is a very serious subject. If you take the humor out of life, all you have left is despair.

The kind of solemnity that denies the essential silliness in all of us has led again and again to self-serving egotism at best, and tragic conflicts – inhumanity – at its worst. It's also lead to the kind of success-oriented religion and culture that implies God can't love a klutz. One of the greatest theologians of all time, Charlie Chaplin understood that.

"Hold it! How did Charlie Chaplin get to be a theologian? He was a comedian!"

Theologian – comedian. Same thing. Comedy is just applied theology, except I don't know any schools that have tumbled to that yet.

In his movies, Chaplin showed us the close relationship between humor and virtues such as faith, hope, and love on the one hand, and between humorlessness and pride, greed and envy on the other hand. He taught us how to laugh at ourselves – how to love our silly, stumbling selves.

In *The Gold Rush*, Chaplin cooks and serves and eats an old boot as if it were the tenderest morsel of French cuisine. If that isn't applied theology, then neither is the Bible.

"You're equating Charlie Chaplin to the Bible?"

We're the only beings on the face of the earth that can laugh. Okay, angels and God can laugh. Humans and angels are the only ones in God's creation endowed with a developed sense of humor. Animals can do almost all the things we can do, and they can even play at a basic sort of level, but they can't get the point of a joke. Animals can express delight, but they can't enjoy a good belly laugh.

That sense of the comic has plenty to do with being created in the "image and likeness of God." It has very little to do with coming up with clever one-liners, or making other people laugh.

"Next thing you're going to say is that God has a sense of humor!"

You got it!

"And the Bible is a joke book?"

The Bible is a joke book.

Pay attention. All of Charlie Chaplin's films use the same basic theme we find in the Bible. All of Chaplin's films are about a funny little guy who keeps falling on his face and who does everything wrong but somehow seems to come out on top in the end.

The first part of the Bible's story is about a funny little band of Hebrews who bumbled their way through history, doing just about everything wrong, but God loved them very particularly and named them the carriers of the promise. Children of the covenant. *Bar and bat mitzvah.*

The second part of the story is about a child who was born in a tiny town on the edge of nowhere, in a barn, who was "despised and rejected." Nobody thought he'd amount to a hill of beans. He didn't. He was executed on a cross on top of a garbage dump. But he was the carrier of a new covenant and the founder of the Christian church that spread to every country in the world. The Bible is classic comedy that turns all our expectations on their heads. Jesus said as much in some great one-liners. "The first shall be last, and the last shall be first." "Unless you become like children, you can't enter God's realm."

"What about you?"

Me?

"Have you got a sense of humor?"

I hope so.

"Well, you'll need it. Because it says in the Bible, 'Don't spit into the wind.' Which is exactly what you are doing. Talk like that will get you branded as a loser and nobody loves a loser."

You're not very bright are you? That's the point of the whole thing. God loves a loser! That's the essential story of all the great religions – of losers who did everything wrong and God, or Allah or Manitou or the Great Spirit loved them anyway. God *especially* loves a loser. It *is* spitting into the wind (which is not in the Bible, by the way). It is tilting at windmills. It's also a long and noble tradition. Buddha. Moses. Jesus. Mohammed. Don Quixote. Charlie Chaplin.

Make your own list and have a good laugh because we are all part of the divine comedy.

The Meaning of It All

Playing God

"Don't try to play God."

It's an unanswerable statement. And really bad advice.

Because that's exactly what we do. It's exactly what we *should* do.

I played God a couple of years ago because I happened to be in the right place at the wrong time. Or perhaps the right time. I was shanghaied by a church school teacher at the top of the basement stairs.

"I need your help. Now!" she said, and led me by the arm into one of the Sunday School rooms. The problem was obvious. Young Peter was dressed as a shepherd for the Christmas pageant, and he was using his shepherd's staff to hold the entire class at bay. He was swinging it around while the rest of the children cowered in a corner.

"Give me that stick!" I ordered from well out of range.

"Go to hell!" said Peter.

I walked closer. Peter swung the staff at me, I caught it in my hand. It hurt. But I hung on and so did Peter. I pulled him toward me, threw both my arms around him, and I held him in a bear-hug while he struggled.

He struggled long and hard and shouted obscenities at me. I simply hung on, my arms wrapped around him. Eventually his struggling and his curses dissolved into tears. He released his hold on the staff and it clattered noisily to the floor. Gradually the bear-hug turned into a human hug.

"You're going to beat the shit outta me, aren't you?" Peter finally asked.

"Why would I do that?"

"Because that's what my dad always does."

"Does he do that often?"

"Yeah. He comes home drunk all the time and beats me and my mom and everybody except the baby."

"I don't want to beat you, Peter. I want to be your friend."

"Nobody wants to be my friend. Whenever I get a friend I hit them and then we're not friends anymore." Peter began to cry again. By this time he was sitting on my lap, my arms still around him, but making no attempt to leave. I wondered if this was the first time he'd ever been cuddled by a man. Did he know that men can love as well as hurt?

"Are they going to kick me out of the church play?" Peter asked.

"We'd like you to be in the church play, Peter. But we don't want you to hit people. Can you promise not to hit people?"

"No," said Peter. I'd never heard such sadness in a child's voice. "No, because I just start hitting when I get something like a stick in my hand."

"Peter," I said. "Maybe I can help. I'll sit right in the front row during the Christmas concert. And when you feel like hitting somebody with your shepherd's staff, you just look at me.

And then we'll both pretend that I'm giving you a nice, warm hug. Do you think that would work?"

Peter and I exchanged knowing glances several times during the performance. And he got through the Christmas concert just fine. And I ached for him and his family, knowing the phone calls that had been made and the interventions that had to happen. Family violence must not be allowed to continue, and sometimes there needs to be the pain of justice, before we see the "Peace on earth!" which the angel in that pageant promised.

On the way home, it came to me. I've been playing God! God doesn't zap with thunderbolts or bully people into decisions. God simply offers love, in all sorts of forms. Christmas, Good Friday and Easter are at the top of the list.

And then God sits there, in the front row of our lives, smiling and encouraging and helping us find the internal strength to do the right thing.

One of those right things is to play God. Just as often as we can.

The Gift of Guilt

"Frank," I asked. "Is that infection in my eye psychosomatic?"

"At some level, yes," he grinned, "but if you came to see me with it, I don't think I'd start asking you questions about your childhood."

But he might have. The sty in my eye got started by a bout of the flu, and the flu was as bad as it was because I was run down, and I was run down because I'm a workaholic, and I'm a workaholic because way deep down inside I still think I have to earn any love or affection I may get, and I caught the bug because I was working in an office where lots of other people had the bug and where people reinforce my workaholism.

It's all connected.

Frank McNair is my friend and psychiatrist. In a conversation recently, Frank said the greatest medical advance of the past decade was the recognition by the medical community that human beings are a single unit. Humans are physical, psychological, social and spiritual creatures, but the divisions between those are quite arbitrary. Everything we are is completely connected.

That doesn't come as a huge surprise to those of us who poke around in the spiritual ballpark. Priests, prophets and sages of every spiritual tradition have been saying that for centuries. Frank has been saying that for as long as I've known him, but he's not typical of most doctors. Standard medical practice has been to treat the disease or malady as if it had no human person attached to it.

It's not hard to get a simple eye infection treated, but a tear in the eye may be much more difficult. Tears of guilt, especially. Especially tears of guilt about things we know are wrong but which we can't seem to change. Like my workaholism.

There are bushels of books on the pop-psyche shelves prescribing ways of escaping guilt, but most of them miss the point. Guilt has many forms of course, and some of it may be misplaced, but fundamentally guilt is good. Guilt is the spirit of God deep inside us whispering, "There's something wrong here. Don't just keep avoiding it. Fix it."

The traditional word for that is "sin," which isn't really a popular concept anymore because it's been trivialized to mean nasty little things we do in the bathroom or behind the barn. Actually, sin doesn't have much to do with being naughty. There are a bunch of things in the traditional "sin" category and they may cause us problems, but that isn't what "sin" is about. Sin is ignoring, suppressing the spirit within us that is telling us we are avoiding some fundamental realities and we are not going to have our life really together until we sort those things out. Until we face up to it and deal with it, we feel guilt.

Guilt is to our spirituality what pain is to our bodies. It tells us something is wrong. Pain is necessary for physical survival – guilt is necessary for spiritual survival.

Psychiatry as a science, cannot deal with guilt, because psychiatry is amoral. It doesn't know about sin. But some psychiatrists like Frank, know that sin is real – that the guilt resulting from sin is a gift of God, that the sin and the guilt must be taken seriously and named as such.

It's been fashionable to remove guilt. Guilt is bad, say many pop-psychologists and therefore should be eliminated. Sometimes that's true. There are whole areas of guilt that are induced by others or by ourselves that can eat us whole. But sometimes guilt is there because we are plain and simply guilty. Something is wrong and it needs fixing.

Repentance, turning around and changing what needs to be changed (sometimes with the help of a psychiatrist) is the appropriate response to guilt. In return, the spirit of God offers the graceful gift of forgiveness.

Good psychiatry is priestly medicine and an integral part of all healing.

The High Cost of Success

Sometimes I feel guilty about not feeling guilty.

It starts with the junk mail. In any week, we get enough junk mail to heat the house all winter.

A bunch of the junk mail is advertising for motivational seminars, events designed to turn a natural slob like me into a highly-motivated, goal oriented, achievement focused, financially successful, well-organized and, I presume, self-satisfied jock. Sales people phone me guaranteeing results I can measure in dollars. (I tell them there are other kinds of results but they have no idea what I'm talking about.)

Sometimes I buy their spiel and I go. I feel intimidated. I pay a couple of hundred dollars to sit in a stuffy hotel meeting room looking at computer generated slides, and come out of it feeling I'm a failure.

Most of the time. Occasionally I come out all pumped up and determined to "maximize my earning power." But it doesn't last. Then I remember the guilt and anxiety I felt in school when I didn't get my homework done and my grade ten teacher would recite:

> *"We must be up and doing, aye each minute.*
> *The grave gives time for rest when we are in it."*

I also hear my dad quoting Rudyard Kipling at me.

> *"If you can fill the unforgiving minute,*
> *with sixty seconds worth of distance run,*
> *yours is the earth and everything that's in it,*
> *and (which is more) you'll be a man, my son."*

It's not that I'm dumb. I know exactly what I should do. The computer on which I am writing this has a program on which I can schedule every minute of every day of my life from now until the year 2099. When I read the sales pitch that comes with that program, I feel guilty about not expecting to live until 2099, and about not wanting to schedule my life like that. So I stick to the good old pocket diary which works fine as long as I remember to write things into it once in awhile and read what's written there.

I watched an interview on TV with a top CEO of a management consulting outfit. He boasted that he had his life completely scheduled for the next four years. Did he get time to spend with his family? "Yes, I've scheduled one day each month when I have a four-hour time block to visit my children." A man I worked with several years ago told me with complete seriousness that, "My wife and I make love on Sunday afternoons at 2:00."

If that's what it takes to be a successful person, I fail.

And the moment I wrote that, I felt guilty because I didn't feel guilty.

Suppose I had done all the things they tell you in those seminars or in those self-help books I read when I feel depressed. I might be living in a large home, with lots of money in mutual funds and no financial concerns whatever.

Make no mistake, I'd love to have all that, but if the price is four scheduled hours with my kids a month and an orgasm on demand at 2:00 p.m. on Sundays – well, the cost is too high.

Maybe I don't take those motivational seminars seriously enough. When I see the strained earnestness in the eyes of the leaders with their designer clothes and studied casualness, I can't help but wonder if they actually believe what they say. I think they think they believe it. They have convinced themselves they believe it. But I wonder if, lying on their bed fighting a headache in the middle of the night, they still believe their own spiel. Or anything else.

No, that's wrong. I shouldn't be so cynical. They have a lot of good stuff to say, and I should straighten up and fly right and get my life together. Organize my time and maximize my efforts.

Well, I try. I really do. But I always find myself doing things because they're fun, or because I think they are necessary or needed, or because I see tears in someone's eyes. Sometimes, when I pay attention, I do things because I feel the gentle hand of God in the small of my back nudging me toward something that doesn't make a bit of sense to those motivational mandarins. Or to me either.

Recently I was reading a book that asked the question, "What single thing has motivated your life?" I couldn't come up with any one single thing. There's been a whole bunch of things. Greed. Selfishness. Pride would have to be in there, if I'm being even partly honest. Occasionally also generosity. Love. And God. Sometimes I have no idea what is motivating me, but there I go.

Am I the only one who can't isolate my motives? Am I unusual because I don't have "career objectives"? I've had all kinds of career fantasies – winning the Decathlon in the Olympics, starring on Broadway, writing a world-class novel, becoming Prime Minister – but I've never been able to pursue any of those for more than a minute or two.

I read about a guy once who was on a really promising career trajectory. He had degrees from all the right schools, and everyone had him pegged to be the new CEO in a couple of years. Out on a road trip one day, he fell on his head, went blind for awhile, and got religion. That got his life all screwed up. He wrote a letter in which he said, "The good things that I want to do, I don't do. The rotten things I don't want to do, I do anyway. My head's all messed up."

His name was Saul in Hebrew, or Paul in Greek, and we call him "Saint," because all this happened more than 1900 years ago, and we have a bunch of his letters in the Bible. Some of them are full of mind-numbing jargon, which goes to show that just because you get religion, it doesn't mean you've got a life. But some of his letters dance and sing and tell you that Paul is a guy you could love. It's almost as if he's two people – the stuffy, bureaucratic academic on one hand, and the dancing, singing lover-of-life on the other.

I understand Paul. I was CEO of a media consulting outfit in New York for awhile, and spent my life signing my name to things I never had time to read and attending meetings with people I didn't know and sometimes didn't like. I left that, came back to Canada with my family, and in a couple of decades found myself doing the same thing all over again in a publishing company.

Typical male. If there's a ladder around I'll try to climb it, even if later I find it's leaning against the wrong wall. I've learned a little bit over the years. Now when those motivational pamphlets come to me I toss them in the vertical file and check out my friend Paul. Because he's not around in person, just in his letters, I can ignore the parts where he's boring and irrelevant and just read those passages where he's singing his fool head off and thoroughly, wonderfully in love with God.

My grade ten teacher, my dad, and all those motivational managers will nod knowingly and tell you that, unfortunately, Ralph was undisciplined and therefore didn't make much out of his life. "Nice guy. Had a bit of talent. But just couldn't get his act together." All true.

So I'll go and talk to Zoë, my granddaughter who is just a year old. She has more basic wisdom than all those successful motivators, and knows what is important in life. Zoë will look at me, snap my red suspenders, stick out her tongue and give them all the old raspberry, and maybe give me a wet, sticky kiss.

When Zoë and I look at each other, we see angels.

And whoever heard of an angel with career objectives and a well-organized date-book?

In Search of Mediocrity

"If you dream hard enough; if you want it badly enough; if you train long enough..."

I was watching the Olympics on TV. They kept spinning that commercial featuring a muscular runner with dedication and commitment written all over his face – oozing out of his pores. Pouncing out of the starting blocks, his face exuded concentration. In slow motion, of course. The commercial was inspirational in the worst sense of the word. And it was selling underarm deodorant.

I enjoy seeing the excellence of physical achievement at the Olympics. There is a kind of perverse pleasure in seeing someone excel at something I can't even imagine attempting. But I have this gremlin on my shoulder asking questions. Why do the TV commentators ask the athletes stupid questions that generate even dumber answers? Why ask athletes any questions at all? Yes, there are a few articulate athletes, but most athletes are at their best when they express themselves through their bodies.

Here are some questions the sports commentators could ask, though it's the commercial sponsors and the Olympic organizers who should answer. "What will the weight lifters, the guys who hoist three times their body weight, look like ten years after they've stopped training?" I know one retired heavyweight lifter. They take him to lunch with a fork lift.

Why not ask, "When you're the best in the world, can you ever love anyone else?"

"What happened to the vast majority of athletes who never get near the Olympics – who were drowned in the wake of these super achievers?" Competitive sport builds confidence along with the muscle, according to the gurus. "Does that include the kid who came last in the first heat of the preliminary trials at the Popkum High School?"

A few years ago I was at a small university where the Hamilton Tiger Cats of the Canadian Football League were having their spring camp. I saw a young man whose neck started at his ears and went sideways at 45 degrees toward his shoulders. "Mom," he said into a pay phone, "I didn't even make the first cut. I'm out, Mom. What am I gonna do? All I know is football."

Well, young man. If you are a real man, that is if you have any testicles left after all those steroids, you'll find yourself a nice flat-chested woman – a failed marathon runner – get a job driving truck and settle down to raise 2.5 children and a dachshund – that is if either of you have any libido left. If you're not sterile. If you can contain your anger and frustration and stay out of jail.

The sports commentators talk about the conquerors, but never about the casualties. Maybe because that's most of us. I'm a sports casualty and so are you, I'll bet, if you think about it. I really, badly, wanted to be a star center in the National Hockey League. I really did, and I would have too, if I hadn't fallen on my face every time somebody passed me the puck. That was in grade three. I was lucky. I had that dream shattered early enough, so I could change the dream to that of pop singer. I didn't make that either.

I was lucky because as an athlete and as a singer I was really awful, right from the beginning, so nobody encouraged me or suggested I undertake training and they certainly didn't offer me a sports scholarship. But our country is full of young men (and a few women) who have had professional sports careers dangled in front of their noses. They have worked and practiced and dreamed their way into superb examples of muscular fitness. Then one day, they hit the glass ceiling. Like the football player at the phone. All they know is sports. There is no place for them to go and they have no other marketable skills.

Competition builds character, they say, and maybe it does for the minority who wind up being winners. For those who turn out, in the end, to be losers, it generally destroys them.

Duane is a man I know very well, who carried his dream of a career in hockey until he was in his early 20s when he actually played semi-pro for awhile. Then he was cut, and took a job pushing paper in a minor office job. He settled on a pro career as a wife abuser and alcoholic couch potato.

In a society where winning is "the only thing," and where rewards come only to those who do really, really well in their "search for excellence," there has got to be a spot for those of us who are just plain mediocre – for those who fall somewhere between the Special Olympics and the real Olympics. That's most of us.

Almost every summer I do a writers' workshop at some retreat center. No, I don't teach writing. I don't know how to write myself. All we do is sit around and share the words we've strung out on a page and wonder why sometimes the words sing and sometimes they suck.

Every one of those workshop people would like to be a famous writer. Me too. Every one of us would like to win the Pulitzer Prize, but mostly we lay the "pullet surprise." I salivate over the poetry of Dylan Thomas and experience little orgasms reading the prose of Annie Dillard. As a writer, I'll never get near them.

The TV commentators and that deodorant commercial are lying. It does not matter how hard you dream or train or want. Some of us just plain don't have the talent or marbles or muscles or skills or whatever. That football player had all the muscles and all the desire, but he was born with two left feet and he tripped over the 20-yard line. I don't have that tiny edge of insanity or genius that makes the difference between a plodder and a prodigy.

We need good truck drivers. If that young football player on the telephone had not been sold a bill of goods about becoming another Joe Namath, he would not have all those muscles now turning to flab and he might indeed settle down very happily to drive truck and raise a family. No fame, but usefulness. Truck drivers hardly ever have to answer questions from lame-brained TV announcers who ask, "And how did you feel driving 48th in that convoy of 49 trucks?" But we need truck drivers far more than we need football jocks. Otherwise they'd never eat an orange in Ottawa or an apple in Atlanta.

We need lots of plain vanilla writers too, folks who are not Ernest Hemingway but who can put one word after another with reasonable competence so we find out what happened at the city council meeting or who said what at the school board. We need preachers who are not Billy Graham who can speak to the needs of a dozen folks at the little white church in Eyebrow, Saskatchewan. We need cooks who are not Julia Child who can whip up a decent mess of bangers and mash for Friday night supper. We need singers who are not Jessie Norman who can sing at the community concert in Plain, Washington.

Instead, we do a good job of honoring the misfits at both ends of the excellence spectrum, but we ignore the majority in the middle, maybe because we are just a little bit boring. But just because we are boring, doesn't mean we are undeserving.

So! Yet another sky blue proposal to reform the world.

In addition to the world Olympics and the Special Olympics (both of which we could live without), I propose the absolutely necessary Mediocre Olympics in which we'll have contests in everything from typing data into computers to child care to truck driving to writing. No medals for those who come first, nor for those who come last, but all the kudos will go to those of us who dream hard but never leave the center of the pack. We're the ones who try just as hard and want it just as bad and really need that sprinter's underarm deodorant.

We're the ones grinding it out in the middle – the ones who keep the world turning.

Mediocrity rules!

Ain't It Awful?

I'm an optimist. I can't help it.

Being an optimist is not popular nowadays, because it's so much more fun to collect bad news and play our favorite parlor game, "Ain't it awful!" Being an optimist is like having a contagious skin disease. Nobody wants you at their party because you spoil the fun. When everybody is having a belly-aching good time, you say something positive and you find yourself being treated like a male stripper at a Pentecostal pray-in.

The media are by nature hyper-pessimistic. They have to be. If you and I do our job, pay our taxes, love our families, etc., we are guaranteed a life of anonymity. Even if I am exceptionally generous, work hard in the community, and give a bunch of money to charity, I won't get more than two or three lines in the "Community Highlights" section. But if I start shooting people on the street,

I am guaranteed the front page. No news is good news, they say, and the reverse is also true. Good news is no news. So we are fed on pessimism, and we collect all the awful stories about crooked politicians (the honest ones don't get coverage) and marauding teen gangs (the teens who stay in school go unnoticed) and come to the conclusion that the world is going to hell in a handbasket.

It's not. But who believes it?

For instance. Almost anybody will tell you there is more and more violent crime. But Canada's violent crime rate has been going down for several years. Especially murder has been going down, and this since we abolished the death sentence.

Go to the library and read some old newspapers from about the turn of the century. You think we have crooked politicians? In the good old days, vote buying was rampant, open, and accepted. Bribery and corruption were simply part of the game. It was expected.

John A. Macdonald, the first Prime Minister of Canada, was a lush. During his long, rambling speeches in parliament, he had flunkies bring him water glasses full of straight gin and he'd be six sheets to the wind and ramble on and on admiring his own eloquence. Everybody knew it. But they reelected him.

Our wartime Prime Minister, William Lyon Mackenzie King, was nuttier than a fruitcake. He held seances so he could talk to his dead mom. He asked his dog for political advice. King wouldn't make it beyond city councilor these days. As soon as any politician runs for a major office, the media sniff around in their past until they find something steamy – he smoked pot in high school, she went skinny dipping on grad night – then paste it all over the tabloids. This media snooping is unfair to many people who may have made petty mistakes years ago, but on the other hand, it also keeps some real shysters out of politics.

The British royal family has shown itself to be remarkably dysfunctional, but so what else is new? Henry VIII was no paragon of virtue. Zoë, an empress of Russia who died in the year 1050, apparently was a virgin until she was 60 then discovered sex and spent the rest of her life making up for lost time. My encyclopedia says her reign was remarkable "for its artistic achievement and the level of corruption." Randy royals are no new phenomenon.

Poverty is still a despicable fact, even in the prosperous nations of the world, but the poor (in economically developed countries at least) are generally far better off than they were even a couple of decades ago. The newspaper, the other day, ran the story of an inquest into two street people found dead in Winnipeg. Both were alcoholics. That's tragic, of course, but the news is that an inquest was held. As a society, we cared enough to ask, "Why did these two people die?"

A story in the *Winnipeg Free Press* from the 1920s reports a particularly cold night when "almost a wagon-load of corpses" was picked up off the streets, which was "considerably more than usual." The story was not about how tragic these deaths were, but simply an illustration of how cold it was. The battle for dignity and decency for the poor among us is by no means over, and I don't mean to minimize their plight. But let's at least give ourselves some credit for taking the problem more seriously.

Most of my female friends, Bev included, are feminists, at least to the extent that they are part of the struggle to gain equality and justice for women. Most of my male friends and I would also call ourselves feminists, if that means we support women in this struggle. Every once in awhile we are knocked back on our keesters by an event that shows us how far we have to go. And we tend to play the "ain't it awful" game around this subject (and others).

But listen. My dear mom was not even legally a person under the law when she was born in 1900. She could not own property, or vote, nor could she be legally responsible for her kids, her own debts, or anything else. Every once in awhile, to see if we've made any progress, we have to look in the rear view mirror.

Spousal violence was not an issue 50 years ago, not because it didn't happen, but because it was simply accepted that papa had to "discipline" the "little woman" along with the children, from time to time. I spent years as a court reporter in the '50s and '60s and I don't recall a single incidence of spousal violence, except when it led to death. Nor was "date rape" even part of our vocabulary. It's not that these crimes didn't happen. It's that we simply accepted them as part of the way things were.

In the Bible, there is an old law: "Thou shalt not kill." We take that to mean anyone, but the early Hebrews who wrote it down only understood it to mean members of their own clan. Same thing with all the other rules. You gained virtue by killing people who were "foreigners." Theirs was a tribal culture, which meant that outside the tribe, anything was fair game if you could get away with it.

The idea that the moral and ethical code applied to your whole country grew very gradually in Europe during the Reformation. It even began to include people from other countries. But not other races. Early settlers in Newfoundland hunted aboriginals for sport. Stalin killed millions of Ukrainians, perhaps more than Hitler killed Jews. Idi Amin tried to wipe out the East Indians. And only a few years ago we had the horror of "ethnic cleansing."

But slowly it is beginning to dawn on us that not all is fair in love and war. Only after the first world war did the concept of "war crimes" come along and only after the second did we begin to act on the concept.

Recently, several Canadian soldiers in Africa on a peacekeeping mission were charged in connection with the death of a Somali civilian. That wouldn't have occurred to the military a few years ago. "A few of the boys got a bit excited. Nothing to worry about. Dismissed."

Meanwhile the concept of international law is growing. Slowly and fitfully, but growing. The Canadian military chaplains recently donated a bunch of money to help the women who had been raped by rampaging soldiers in eastern Europe. The soldiers' freedom to rape used to be considered a legitimate fringe benefit.

However bumbling the attempts, the fact that the United Nations is taking a hand in the enforcement of human rights is a move in the right direction. Even in the United States, the only superpower left in the world, more and more people are questioning the right or the wisdom of America playing the role of world police.

Our concept of law and justice has grown over the millennia since Moses' ten commandments were handed down. Now people of faith are speaking the words from Mount Sinai to the whole world. "Thou shalt not kill" applies, not only to people of other tribes, not only to people of other countries, not only to people of other races, but to the whole world ecosystem.

Most people don't go that far. Not yet. But the idea is taking hold and growing. Some theologians are even talking about the universe as "God's body."

The killing has not stopped. But for more and more people throughout the world, killing is *seen to be wrong*. And that is progress. There is room for a little bit of judicious optimism. Instead of round after round of "ain't it awful" we could handle the occasional chorus of "ain't it wonderful?" In the long run, humanity is making progress.

If nothing else, a bit of optimism helps cut through the soul-shriveling cynicism. And it makes socializing a whole lot more fun.

We've come a long, long way. And yes, we still have a long, long way to go. But from time to time let's drink a toast to what has been gained in our human struggle to become civilized.

Let's Hear It for Laziness

Have you ever heard a speech or read a book in favor of laziness?

Neither have I. But I know a half dozen clergy who could preach a sermon on it, if they wanted to. Not because they are lazy themselves, but because they are the kind of open-minded folks who can look at something that everyone else automatically dumps on and say, "Hey there's something interesting here. Maybe even something worth doing some work on."

I have a confession to make here. I own some big boys' toys and I enjoy fooling around with them. The toys are called computers, and my friends and I play with them – often late at night when everyone else is asleep. It's really just an international electronic play-room, in spite of all the ballyhoo about the World Wide Web. The technology is awesome but most of the conversation is not.

One particularly mind-numbing night, I thought I'd stimulate the gray cells of some of my clergy friends in various parts of the world by asking them if they could develop a "theology of laziness." There was an initial scurrying to their Bibles to see what they could find, but it didn't amount to much. The clerics claimed to be too lazy to spend much time researching a theology of laziness. Fat chance! They're workaholics, every last one of 'em, and were far too busy doing "important" stuff. I felt like the guy who organized a protest march against apathy, but nobody came.

The exception to all of the above was Rev. Deborah Laing (at that time from Rock Island, Quebec, now of North Vancouver, BC) who did some "biblical research." This is what she sent me.

- Luke 12:27 "Consider the lilies, how they grow; they neither toil nor spin..."
- Job 2:11-13 "Now when Job's three friends heard of all this evil that had come upon him, they came each from his own place,...And they sat with him on the ground seven days and seven nights, and no one spoke a word to him..."
- Isaiah 40:30-31 "Even youths shall faint, and be weary, and young men shall fall exhausted; but they who wait for the Lord shall renew their strength..."
- Lamentations 3:25-26 "The Lord is good to those who wait...to the soul that seeks him. It is good that one should wait quietly for the salvation of the Lord."
- Deuteronomy 5:14 "The seventh day is a Sabbath to the Lord your God; in it you shall not do any work, you or your son or your daughter, or your manservant, or your maidservant, or your ox, or your ass, or any of your cattle, or the sojourner who is within your gates, that your manservant and your maidservant may rest as well as you."
- 1 Samuel 19:24 "And he too stripped off his clothes, and he too prophesied before Samuel, and lay naked all that day and all that night."

"I could go on," Deborah wrote, "but it seems rather self-defeating to put a lot of work into a treatise on laziness."

Well no. Kids, I think, can teach us a whole lot about creative laziness.

Some friends of ours own a hot tub. At the end of the day, the whole family spends 15 minutes together soaking. The kids simply enjoy it. The adults feel guilty because, well, "most people don't own hot tubs and isn't this a bit of a self-indulgent luxury? Besides, there are so many important things we should be doing."

I think that's where the theology of laziness comes in. Kids understand it's important to know how to be lazy. There are times to just lie on your back in the sunshine and soak up God's warmth. There are times to simply luxuriate in the long and loving hug of a good friend. The old preacher in Ecclesiastes was right. There is a "time to weep and a time to laugh, a time to mourn and a time to dance."

There are two kinds of insufferable people in the world – those who can't see the pain of the world and refuse to do anything about it, and those who can see nothing else. Balance is the key. There's a time to work your everlovin' butt off and a time to goof off. If you don't get the two in the right proportions, you will end up either a burned-out workaholic or a socially irresponsible slob.

There is a time to soak in hot tubs and a time to work on issues of justice, but they are not the same times.

In her scripture collection on laziness, Deborah might have included the story about the woman of the streets who came in and poured expensive perfume on Jesus' feet. This was at a dinner party, and everyone at the affair dumped on Jesus and the woman.

Well, tough, said Jesus in effect. There is a time to pour costly perfume on people's feet and a time to be out there campaigning for social justice. The big issues will not go away. "We will have the poor still with us," Jesus said to the self-righteous crowd at that dinner party. But for the moment, let the perfume fill our nostrils – let the beauty of the moment fill our souls – and don't be so intentional – so dysfunctionally adult.

When I see a rose, it is my job – no, my holy calling – to stop and enjoy its beauty and to smell its fragrance. Nothing else. For the few seconds I am smelling the rose I must be totally absorbed in it. But if all I do is smell roses, I would be a very sick social parasite.

When I meet someone or something I love, I should express my love. When I see someone in need, I should do what I can to address that need. Loving yourself and loving your neighbor are part of the same package.

No "yes, but..." Psalm 126 wants our "mouths to be filled with laughter."

When you've been given a gift, enjoy it. Indulge in it. Be lazy for a little. And just say, "Thanks!"

When the Game Is Being Played

Funny thing about some sports. Football and hockey for instance. The clock only runs when the game is being played. When you're standing around, waiting for things to happen, the clock stops.

Do you suppose the thing we call maturity is our emotional and spiritual clock that only runs when we're actually living life? I mean really living, as opposed to marking time?

That's an interesting phrase. "Marking time." Standing or lying around vacantly. Nothing much happening in heart or head. Life is on "hold."

That's necessary sometimes, of course. Some people do it too much and others too little. Very few get the right balance.

Look at the faces of people marking time on the plane or subway. Nice faces, but there's no one home. The mind and spirit are turned off.

That's not necessarily bad. We need that sometimes. Sometimes we need to rest and give the body or the mind a bit of time to heal. There is a time to simply vegetate.

I watch football games. And hockey. When I've been hit by life-shattering pain, I may spend hours, almost days watching sports on television which at other times would bore me silly. Sometimes when I'm just plain bushed, I flick on the television and the basic, simple-mindedness of sports plays into my consciousness like music on the telephone when you're on hold.

It's a soft and easy place to stay. I could spend my life there on the couch, a tiny corner of my mind occupied by the minor variables of who wins what and by how much, and thus avoid the painful complexity of life. I could do that. I could sit there and get older by the day without ever growing – except around my waistline – without ever opening my eyes wide with wonder.

I know people who have done that. They reach great age, but remain emotional and spiritual infants. Their conversation runs no deeper than, "How about them Blue Jays, eh?"

Our maturity clock runs only when we really live. We grow inside when we're laughing, crying, thinking lively thoughts, working at something worth doing, genuinely relaxing, dreaming real dreams, making love, playing like a child...

Love Is a Choice

I'm hopping mad.

And it's hard to write about love when you're blazing inside – when you can't get your mind off the delicious image of a certain person strung up by his toenails. Or better still, suspended by an even more tender part of his anatomy.

For the past ten minutes I have been writing a stream of invective, and it felt good. I erased it because it was totally libelous, and because I found my fingers typing stuff about cooling down and seeing things from his point of view.

That's the problem with calling myself a writer. I'm really just a typist. I sit here and my fingers move and I read what comes up on the screen and I wonder who said that. Me?

At least, sometimes that's the sensation. Some writer friends tell me this is a kind of prayer. The words sometimes seem to come from so deep inside that I know God must be involved in those words somehow. They are not things I have "thought," at least consciously.

This all began because I edit a journal called *Aha!!!* which offers resources for preachers. The theme of the week was "love" and so I had to say something about love. Hack writers don't just get to pen the sweet musings of their mind on a spring morning, tra la. We have to write as per schedule, as per topic, as per whatever is on for that day. So I am supposed to write about love while I'm furious at someone?

Get real! How can you talk about love when you're seething?

The reasons for my anger are not that important, except to say that I feel I've been had. I've been diddled – led down the garden path and betrayed with broken promises and duplicity. But still, I have some really strong convictions that say I am required to love this person for the simple reason that we are fellow human beings.

Really? Says who?

But now, even though I don't want them to, words appear on my screen, typed by my fingers. "Is it possible he feels betrayed by me?"

Not only possible, but probable. "Is there any way I can see things from his perspective?"

No. Not now. Time will dilute my anger, and then perhaps. Not now.

"Love this man," say my fingers.

No, absolutely not. Right now I am nursing a good mad so back off.

Then at least don't add fuel to the flames! Don't follow the impulse that says, "Phone him up and yell!" Don't write the letter that would destroy him or you.

"Love one another," says Jesus. No ifs, buts or maybes.

Not possible, unless loving, for me, right now, at this moment, is simply to back off! Count to 10. Cool it. Walk away until the anger behind my eyes has dissolved. For now, that's the only part of loving I can manage.

Love is making choices, say my fingers. Backing off – giving yourself time – right now that's the loving thing to do.

Tomorrow, "Love one another!" will mean something more.

Enough Is Too Much

My two sisters were saying goodbye to me at the Winnipeg airport. "You never stay long enough," said Verna.

"If I stayed long enough, it'd be too long," I said. "Like in showbiz. Always leave 'em wanting more."

I'd been in Winnipeg making speeches and was told by a few enthusiastic listeners that "You didn't talk nearly long enough." Best compliment a speaker can get. If they'd said, "You spoke just the right length," I would have considered it a criticism. Any speaker, any entertainer, any preacher who knows their business will stop well before the audience wants them to stop.

Some wise sage once said, "Be careful what you ask for. You may get it."

I've always felt I never had enough time to read. I have a whole shelf full of unread books and I yearn for the time to get at them. But I also remember a conversation with a man who found himself quadriplegic after a car accident. "I always wanted enough time to read," he said sadly. "Now I have it."

Another acquaintance loved to play golf. Before he retired, he would play three times a week, and always looked forward to the weekends when he could hit the links. Then he retired and bought a house on the 7th hole of one of those developments built right around a golf course. The price of the house included membership in the club. At last, he could play as much as he wanted to. And he did. Three games a day, sometimes.

It killed him, I think. Golf became an obsession for him as he played more and more. A fine game though it is, golf simply doesn't have enough juice in it to squeeze out a life. He became bored and frustrated, but he had given up everything for this life of golf, so in desperation, he played more and more. Finally he gave up and simply died.

Every one of us has fantasized about having "enough" money. You can see that fantasy in the faces of people lining up to buy lottery tickets. The hunger in their eyes shows the yearning to have enough...enough money for all those dreams. It's not the small prizes they are after. Those are just teasers designed to seduce them into buying more tickets. Which they do, and eventually some of them (fortunately, not most of them) win.

It destroys them. Study after study has shown that a few years after the big win, the folks who have cashed in on the lottery not only have failed to find the happiness they sought, they are usually back to where they started, economically. In the process of soaring up and crashing down, they have often destroyed their family relationships, lost their friends, and given up the job that enabled them to buy the lottery ticket in the first place. For just a little while they had enough. And it was too much. Apparently only those who already have a bundle and are used to living with money can handle winning a couple of million.

I love my middle-aged "kids" and my young grandkids, and Bev and I hunger for more time with them. I like to think the feeling is mutual. If we ever get to the point of finding enough time to be with each, that will be a big, big danger signal. When they're glad to see mom and dad leave, we'll have stayed way too long. "Do you have to go now? Couldn't you stay longer?" are essential words in any family relationship.

I yearn for the day when I'll have enough time to read all those books. It would be wonderful to have the money to go see all those "faraway places with the strange sounding names" that have been calling me. And I have a head full of ideas that bounce around in my brain trying to find their way into print.

It's not likely I'll win the lottery, because I've never bought a ticket in my life. I think lotteries are an evil seduction of people who can least afford to be preyed on by our governments. But a few years back a friend bought Bev and me a ticket as a gift, and that stimulated a couple of fantasies. The fantasy would have turned into a nightmare and the friend into a foe if in fact we had won.

It depends, of course, on what we mean by "enough." I've always had enough to meet my needs. I've had enough food to eat. The house I lived in provided good shelter. I have been loved by my family and my friends. Come to think of it, I have had more than enough. I've lived in abundance.

I've had enough to satisfy my needs but not all my wants. And those wants keep expanding. I'm not likely to find enough time to do the reading and writing I yearn for because each project opens up new doors. I'm never going to live in the house I want because there's always somebody with a bigger, better, newer house that I will want. But the house I live in is certainly enough. More than enough.

If you ever hear me saying, "I've got everything I want," please fold my hands gently across my chest and put a couple of quarters on my eyelids. If I'm not physically dead, I will certainly be spiritually dead.

Every human being deserves and needs to have enough to live in dignity and peace.

Beyond that, let's be careful what we ask for.

If we ever have enough to fulfill our wants, it will be too much and it will destroy us.

A Tree by a River

I live in the Okanagan Valley, a long rain-shadow just east of the western coastal range of mountains. It stretches up into BC and down into Washington State where it changes a vowel and becomes the Okanogan.

The valley is a semi-desert. It's cloudy a lot in the winter, but the clouds don't produce much rain. And in the summer it is hot and dry. Can't grow much except Ponderosa pines and bunch grass.

Except that many years ago a missionary priest, Fr. Pandosy, wandered through this valley, and brought some small apple trees with him. (The Johnny Appleseed legend notwithstanding, you don't grow decent apples from seeds.) The first apples were planted by a creek that flows near our house. The first tender little trees were watered by hand from the creek till their taproots found the water level, and then the trees grew big and strong. A scion or cutting from the original apple tree Fr. Pandosy planted still grows and bears fruit in the valley.

For lunch today I had a big red apple, a delicious descendant of that first tree that priest planted many years before I was born. Fr. Pandosy didn't come here mainly to plant apples, of course. He came to share his faith with the people who already lived here, but I think the apple trees became a symbol of that faith.

I wonder if Fr. Pandosy was thinking of that ancient poem by Jeremiah when he dug into the sandy soil by the creekside? Perhaps he read:

> *"They shall be like a tree planted by water,*
> *sending out its roots by the stream.*
> *It shall not fear when the summer heat comes*
> *and its leaves shall stay green;*
> *in the year of drought it is not anxious,*
> *and it does not cease to bear fruit."*

Recently, walking through the hills, I came across an abandoned farm. Near the house was an apple tree, still alive, but bearing only a very few, tiny, wormy apples. The tree desperately needed two things. Water and pruning.

I have no doubt Fr. Pandosy pruned his apple trees. If you don't prune an apple tree it will grow huge quantities of tiny, inedible apples. And when I say pruning, I mean pruning. To those of us who don't understand apple trees, it seems like a cruel and merciless hacking away at the limbs. But you don't get good fruit without vigorous pruning.

Fr. Pandosy knew that suffering, pain and struggle by them-selves don't produce fruitful people, any more than pruning an apple tree will, of itself, produce good fruit. Folks who get beaten by life or circumstances are stunted, twisted or destroyed. Apple trees that are simply pruned will die, unless they are planted by a stream. Or the stream is brought to the tree through irrigation. There needs to be water, nourishment to feed that tree or the pruning will kill it. Trees and humans can handle almost any-thing and grow in the process, if their roots go deep into the soil of community and the water of the Spirit.

Blessings come when our taproots grow deep in the nour-ishing soil and life-giving water of our spirituality, and our lives are pruned as we care and sacrifice for others.

Then, like Fr. Pandosy's apple trees, our roots can go deep into the water of life and we are blessed.

We bear good fruit.

A Wasteful God

An ocean breeze teases my graying hair, and I glance up from my deck chair to see the world of ocean, shore and sky around me. Suddenly I notice a single gnarled pine on a tiny bit of rock off the end of an island. Around it the evening mists melt in soft shades of gray and blue and green and orange and pink blending into nameless shades that silhouette my tiny tree. I catch my breath at the glory of it. I want to yell at all the cruise-ship passengers, "Look! Look at this gift of beauty God is giving you."

Two deck chairs down a man in a T-shirt that says, "I golf for food," is telling another man about his daughter's slob boyfriend down in Hoboken. These men don't see, and neither do the others, they are so absorbed in ordinariness. There are so many trees and so many rocks and islands and there is mist all over. Who would notice this one jeweled moment?

But over by the rail, a middle-aged woman brings her hand up to her face. She sees it too. I walk up to stand nearby. "Wow!" I say. "Yeah," she says. For an instant, we are in a sanctuary – total strangers sharing intimate and holiest communion.

God wastes a coastline full of trees and rocks and sunsets on a boatload full of jaded tourists so that one neurotic writer and one nameless woman can *see* God together. A tiny moment, then she goes off and I go off. God knows the preciousness of words and trees and rocks, and wastes them, hoping, longing for people touristing through life to stop and notice.

"Nice scenery around here, eh?" says the man in the T-shirt.

His comment angers me for some reason though I say nothing. But a phrase pops out from somewhere in the folds of memory. "Out, out, brief candle..."

I remembered sitting in the dark in Ashland, Oregon, seeing that play two years ago. I wondered then and wonder now how many in that audience heard the bright agony in that holy speech.

> *Life's but a walking shadow; a poor player,*
> *That struts and frets his hour upon the stage,*
> *And then is heard no more; it is a tale*
> *Told by an idiot, full of sound and fury,*
> *Signifying nothing.*

I heard an actor say those words which I had heard before but never really noticed. This time the actor spoke and I could hear the wonderful futility of life – together that actor and I touched the pain that tells us we are mortal; pain that cuts the wound that makes us whole and holy so that we knew we are created in the image and the likeness of a weeping God.

Every writer, since Shakespeare penned those words, has struggled to express such sacred, concentrated truth with promiscuous contaminated words – has hoped and prayed that with the blunt instruments of verbs and nouns and adjectives, the thinking, feeling soul may be exposed and health restored.

Sometimes, in the joyful confluence of word and insight, truth and beauty are expressed and heard. And when two or three have gathered and can touch that truth together, then for a sacred moment even total strangers share the holiest communion.

And in that instant, all creation sings.

Bombs and Gifts

It was a flight from New York to Toronto. A bit bumpy. Just enough to make you aware of your stomach.

Then, BAM! And a flash of brilliant light!

There were screams and gasps. Then nothing. We just kept flying right along as if everything was quite normal. Eventually (it seemed like hours later) a laconic pilot spoke over the loudspeaker.

"You may have noticed a slight noise and bit of a flash a few moments ago," he drolled. "Nothing to worry about. We were hit by lightning."

Nothing else. No explanations. We're sitting there white-faced and shaking, and that's all we get from the pilot.

I'm always interested in what happens to me when I catch a glimpse of my own death. This time, the first thing that came into my head was, "Well, if I'm going to die, I'm going to en-joy it."

That's all! And I'm still trying to figure out what I meant.

I was flying out of Kelowna on an assignment for a magazine. The seat belt sign had just gone off, and I was gazing at the mountains where loggers had cut huge bald spots along the ridges. The flight attendant was smiling her way up and down the aisle with plastic cups of lukewarm coffee, when the pilot suddenly stood the plane on its wing tip in a quick U-turn back to Kelowna – which emptied most of the coffee cups and several stomachs.

"Ladies and gentlemen," said a very flustered voice on the loudspeaker, "we're going back to Kelowna, and...and...as soon as the plane hits the ground...I mean as soon as the aircraft has landed...get out as fast as you can and don't try to take any luggage or anything with you and for goodness sake, KEEP CALM."

It was the longest trip home I've ever been on. The flight attendants kept walking up and down the aisle smiling broadly through clenched teeth. Nobody was talking.

Me? I wasn't frightened. I wasn't worried. Not a bit of it.

I was terrified!

Pure, utter, unvarnished scared. I could feel my heart pounding against my ribs. I was panting as if I had just run a mile, and squeezing the armrest till it yelped.

It was a bomb scare, we found out later. Some poor demented soul had phoned in a threat. And while most of us were sure it was a hoax, we were still glad the airline was taking it seriously.

A couple of hours later, after a thorough search, we were on our way again. And then I had time to think a little – to reflect on the feelings I'd experienced when that aircraft was rushing home to safety.

I had been afraid all right. But after several minutes, the terror gave way to a kind of peacefulness, and I found myself wondering if this really was the end of my life.

Well, no, the terror didn't give way. It was still there. But on top of that fear, or beside it, I found I wasn't afraid of death. In the middle of that fear, I found peace.

Looking back over my life, I knew it had at least been worth living. I was grateful for the loved ones in my life – Bev, my children – and a quiet, wordless prayer formed inside me. It was a prayer for those I would leave behind. It was gratitude for the life I would leave. And thanks for the life I knew would follow.

Even fear brings its gifts.

High Altitude Tears

Here I am on Air Canada flight 117 and I'm bawling like a baby. I'm trying to figure out why.

Why do I cry at high altitudes? Do large-nosed people need more oxygen?

The trigger in this instance was a movie short. It was about Yousuf Karsh, the renowned photographer. I've always appreciated Karsh's photos. I think I'd like Karsh as a person. He had a big nose.

Those of us with big noses learn as teenagers what others learn two decades later. You don't get love from good looks.

When I take a snapshot, I focus on the nose. Karsh gets the soul in focus. It's been said that God's glory is a person fully alive. Karsh, for the most part, shows us people fully alive. Most of them are 60 plus. There are wrinkles and lines and deep shadows under the eyes. There's soul in there.

I have wrinkles and lines too. Also bags under my eyes. The nose has enlarged pores and one or two exuberant blood vessels. The whole thing reminds people of the harvest moon. But there's a soul in there. I know my tears come from my soul, even though I don't really know what a soul is.

I think I saw it once. A soul that is. When I saw Karsh's portrait of the great contralto Marian Anderson, for a moment I saw the face of God. I met Marian Anderson once, years ago. She was a big woman. She had large, working-woman's hands. I was a neophyte radio reporter trying so hard to make an impression. Marian Anderson answered the profound questions I didn't have the wit to ask. She looked at me the way my mother used to look at me.

Maybe that's what soul is. The face of God shining through people. When we let it.

The movie showed us a session of Karsh photographing Leonard Bernstein. Bernstein was an irascible old SOB who smoked too much, drank too much, pushed people around and had an ego the size of the 767 I'm flying in. But Bernstein was a passionate genius and a man of God. I don't know if Bernstein knew he was a man of God, but he was.

Bernstein's *West Side Story* is a sermon on reconciliation and death. *West Side Story* is another retelling of the noblest of all myths. One dies that others may live.

The Karsh film ended with a remarkable sequence of stills, people who had lived an abundant spiritual life. Pablo Picasso. Marian Anderson. Albert Einstein. Eleanor Roosevelt. Martin Luther King. And the music behind those stills was from Bernstein's *West Side Story*. "There's a place for us... Somewhere...Somehow."

Air Canada is taking me home from Frankfurt. I've been at the *Buch Messe*, the world book fair. It's a pretty rarefied atmosphere, there among all those international publishers.

Too rarefied sometimes. Publishers tend to smoke too much and Germans tend to smoke too much and German publishers have never known what it's like to breathe oxygen. You can be overwhelmed and choked up in more ways than one.

"The largest and oldest book fair in the world," the organizers call it.

"Oldest" I have confirmed by my historian friend Gerald Hobbs who says Martin Luther referred to it in his writings.

"Largest?" Well I can't imagine anything much larger. Think of a room the size of a football field. There's row upon row of publishers' stalls full of books. Now imagine three floors like that. Then visualize four buildings like that. Literally a forest of books. That's the Frankfurt Bookfair.

In that massive bookfair, our publishing company had two three-foot shelves. Ten books. I couldn't tell if it was the smoke from all the cigarettes or that thought which got me choked up.

I look out the airplane window. The clouds have cleared from below us. I can see miles of lakes and trees. I wonder if there are enough trees left in the world for next year's *Buch Messe*.

The view from my window reminds me of a vacation up high in the mountains behind Banff. I'm sitting on a rock, just at the tree line, feasting on a panorama of valley and lake and forest. I look down and at my feet is a tiny pine tree. Three inches tall. At that altitude it might make four inches before it is crushed by snow or destroyed by the cold. But the pine tree struggles. All of God's great urge to life is there in that little pine tree.

The rock on which I'm sitting is decorated by a primitive lichen and beside the lichen a fossilized sea shell. A tiny creature that struggled for life and then died a million or more years ago.

Tears sting in the cold mountain air. There's something huge, profound in that fossil and that tree and that vista. There's God in that. And questions.

Was it worth it for that sea creature? Is it worth it for that tiny tree? Are those ten books worth it?

Did God put that sea creature there or plant that struggling pine so that a middle-aged hiker with tired feet and aching soul might catch a glimpse of God? Was it worth it for God?

Is it possible that somewhere, someone else with an aching heart might read one of those ten books and catch a glimpse of God? Books have a shorter life span than tiny trees. Do they justify the sweat and the risk and the work? Do they justify cutting down the trees? I desperately need to believe they do.

I talked to Bev on the phone last night. She'd been to see the doctor in the afternoon. The news was good. It was only gallstones. For weeks we'd both lived with the fear that every middle-aged person faces. What if it's cancer? Bev is now older than her mother was when she died of cancer.

Maybe my tears up here on the airplane are left over from last night. Bev has struggled long and hard and for the most part, faithfully. Mothering four kids isn't easy. Pastoring a congregation isn't easy. God knows being married to a big nosed egotist like me hasn't been easy. Was it worth it for her?

When you get past 50 you wonder about such things. You spend more time looking back over your shoulder to see where you've been. Does any of it matter?

We had a cherry tree in our back yard. One year, after I'd fussed over it, pruned it, fertilized it and worried over it, it produced a crop of six cherries, and small ones at that. But my, those cherries were sweet.

Six cherries. Four kids. Ten books.

In Toronto, on the way home, a young woman I had never met before said, "I'm not going to tell you why or how, but one of the books you published turned my life around. Thanks." She gave me a hug and walked away.

Jim gave me a hug when he dropped me off at the Toronto airport. "Take care, brother," he said.

Bev will give me a hug when I arrive at the Kelowna airport, and a kiss when we get home.

I look out the airplane window and I'm crying again. I wonder what the stewardess thinks.

I'd like to tell her that I'm not unhappy. I'm not in pain. Well, yes I am, but there's joy in the pain.

"There's a place for us...hold my hand and we're halfway there..."

Thank you Yousuf Karsh.
Thank you Marian Anderson.
Thank you Leonard Bernstein.
Thank you young woman, whoever you are.
Thank you Jim.
Thank you Bev.
Thank you God.

How to Sleep through a Sermon

To Speak, to Dream, to Sleep, ahhhh

There are lots of things you can learn in church, and one of them is the fine art of sleeping through a speech. In church we call it a sermon of course, but the survival techniques are the same as they might be for the Rotary Club or a regional sales meeting. But the learning can be dangerous because there's nothing a speaker dreads more than the sight (or worse, the sound) of someone sleeping through every syllable of poignant prose. Believe me, I know!

The best people to talk to about this art are choir members. Especially in churches where the choir is up front right behind the pulpit for everyone to see. To do it up there, you have to be good at it. I've known people who can spend twenty minutes looking wide awake and interested, when in fact they are sound asleep.

My usual spot is in the back row – the bass section. For many years, Bev's spot was in the pulpit, which was located so she had a clear view of the choir. She was the minister, and once in awhile, a combination of a late night on Saturday and one of her least-best sermons found my eyelids getting heavy. It took finesse and courage for me to doze through one of those homilies.

One of my favorite techniques I call the "thinker's pose." I put my right hand across my forehead, and my right elbow on my right knee. I got the idea from the sculpture by Auguste Rodin called *The Thinker*. It works moderately well, but if you doze too deeply, you can pitch forward and find yourself lying across a contralto's lap.

I didn't sleep often in Bev's sermons because they were generally interesting. Besides, if she caught me sleeping through the sermon in church, I didn't sleep through the one in the car going home.

In churchly circles, there's a whole folklore around people sleeping through sermons. These include comments such as, "if all the people who sleep through sermons were laid end to end, they'd be a lot more comfortable."

And there are hundreds of stories. Bruce Misener, who once served a congregation in Willowdale (ten minutes by bike or five hours by car from Toronto) was a veterinarian before studying theology. Once, while discussing the question of euthanasia, he remarked, "When I was a vet, I used to put animals to sleep every day."

To which someone promptly responded, "Now he only does it on Sunday mornings."

Dave Lovewell had an elderly gentleman who arrived every Sunday, sat himself down in the front pew, and went to sleep during the first sentence of the service and snoozed right through to the end. Occasionally he would let out a loud, sermon-stopping snore that brought the house down laughing.

"It's probably the most peaceful hour of his week," Dave would say philosophically. "And he never fails to compliment me on the sermon." When the old man died, Dave genuinely missed seeing him there, open-mouthed and head back in the front pew. "He kept me honest and humble."

There's one story about a cleric who put his congregation into such a deep sleep, when he came back the next Sunday they were still all there, snoring away. And there are even stories about clergy who have slept through their own sermons. It can happen.

I'm not clergy, but from time to time I'm asked to fill in when a congregation gets really desperate. Preaching at a nearby church one Sunday, I was handed a cassette tape at the end of the service. "We taped your sermon," I was told.

I took it home, had a good lunch, sat down with a cup of coffee in the living room, and popped the tape into the machine. Five minutes into my own sermon I was dead asleep. When Bev walked into the room and saw me, head back, mouth open, snoring my way through my own pious pronouncements, it was her guffaws that woke me up.

One of the talks I often dig out of my sermon barrel is called, "How to listen to the sermon." What I say applies to any speech anywhere. It's not what the speaker says that's important – it's what goes on in your own head. Even a deadly dull presentation can turn into something creative if you turn on the imaginative juices and think of all the things the speaker might have said about the subject.

Dull speakers can't be dull all by themselves. They need dull listeners to accomplish that. Similarly, inspiring speakers can't be inspiring by themselves. They need imaginative listeners.

Sometimes, of course, you are utterly worn out and maybe what you need more than anything is a few minutes of shut-eye. In that case, it's okay to sleep.

But try not to sit in the front row.

And don't snore.

Winning Is Everything!

The greatest religious festival is not Easter. Or Christmas.

The greatest religious festivals are the Grey Cup, the World Cup, the Superbowl, the World Series, the Stanley Cup.

The faithful flock to their holy temples for these – the holiest of our high festivals. There they revere the holy prophet Vince Lombardi who declared unto the faithful that "Winning isn't the only thing. It's everything!" St. Vince thus articulated the first and only commandment of the faithful. "Thou shalt not lose. Ever." (Losers get dropped from the lineup, then from the team, and finally from life itself – and spend their years in couch potato purgatory drinking beer and watching sports on TV.)

When the faithful are assembled for this service of worship and praise, flags, flasks and other votive paraphernalia in hand, the ritual begins. The forces of good (our side) are arrayed against the forces of evil (them) for the ritual struggle. The theologians of this religion, also known as sports reporters, describe every detail and nuance of this ritual, studying every statistic, probing every probability, analyzing every angle.

The thousands physically present in the cathedral (also known as the stadium or bowl or coliseum) raise their voices in praise and thanksgiving as the priests of this religion assemble on the field. The millions watching on TV refill their sacramental vessels with beer and chips, tell the kids and the wife to be quiet, then settle down into the softness of the sofa for this period of meditation and worship.

The ritual begins. The priests, known in this cult as players, reenact an ancient rite, following rubrics known only to the faithful, handed down from father to son from generation unto generation in the sacred scripture – the Rule Book. The Rule Book is enforced by the Bishops (called Referees or Umpires) who may prescribe a period of penance, or sometimes excommunication for those who sin.

The rite, or the game (to use the more common euphemism), is enacted with great enthusiasm and passion, each of the priests and bishops and all of the watching faithful believing firmly that how this is done, and who does it best, really matters. The world will be a better place or a worse place depending on the resolution – the final score.

The worshippers, also known as fans, will hang on their every sacred word, knowing how deeply and profoundly a game being played half a continent away affects their very life. The faithful hunger for real understanding. Statistics.

The theologians explain the more subtle points. "Well, the Sharks are down three to nothing, so they're gonna hafta score some goals if they wanna get back in the game."

Just as in some other religious assemblies phrases such as "Hallelujah" and "Praise the Lord" spring spontaneously from the worshippers' lips, so in the religion of sports, phrases such as "Holy ____," or "Jesus Christ" spring spontaneously to the lips of the faithful, along with other ritual exclamations such as "Kill the SOB."

Young males who feel called to this priesthood (women are unworthy) must offer their bodies as a living and holy sacrifice. Though many are called, few are chosen, and even those often falter during their novitiate, unable to receive their ordination (the draft). They have played too often through their injuries and, before they finish puberty, they have fallen from grace and are unable to play at all.

During their novitiate, many become chemical celibates, trading their sexuality for muscle bulk in the secret priestly rite of steroid injection. The muscle bulk serves them briefly, then they too are sacrificed on the high altar of the draft cut. Although these rejected seminarians may find themselves in couch potato purgatory, they never doubt their faith, and generously offer their wealth, their lives, their health, their families, in their devotion to the faith of their fathers. They attend worship daily at the TV set, and purchase votive objects such as trading cards, sweaters and caps and even season tickets.

They do not resent the chosen few who are elevated to the status of high priest or superstar. To them goes laud and honor and glory and riches. And when injury and steroids destroy even these, they are canonized. They become the saints, their visage and their sacred relics hung in the Hall of Fame.

From generation unto generation, fathers take their sons in pilgrimage to this most sacred shrine. With breaking voices and trembling fingers, they point to these saints of sport, saying, "Believe it, son. That was a real man."

Never the Same Thing Twice

I stood on a street corner in Jerusalem talking with a Jewish friend who told me there were "hundreds, maybe thousands of Jewish sects and they have one thing in common. All of them are convinced all the others are doing it wrong."

In the Christian church, there are over 22,000 denominations.

I don't know how many different kinds of Moslems there are, but it's a bunch. Buddhists and Hindus come in a wonderful variety. And then there's all the colorful aboriginal religions. The "New Age" movement invents new religions daily.

I've heard dozens of sermons and speeches and read umpteen articles and books about how terrible this is. The media folks have a field day pointing accusatory fingers and jumping to the conclusion that since spiritual people can't all be "right" they must all be "wrong."

I've had good Christians telling me Jesus is up there in heaven bawling his eyes out wondering what went wrong – twenty-two thousand variations on what seems, on the face of it at least, a simple message.

But just a darn minute. How many different kinds of people are there? Well, whatever the world's population is today, that's how many different kinds there are. Even identical twins are not identical. Not even any two mosquitoes are identical. No two trees or dandelions – or anything else for that matter – are exactly the same.

So if the Creator never does anything twice, why should that Creator be upset when humans get imaginative and invent new religions?

Christian churches are growing at a rate of 64,000 new Christians every day – most of that in Africa. And there are 65 new Christian congregations formed every day. Which should be good news, except that at the turn of the century, there were 1,900 Christian denominations. Now there are 22,000.

That's five new denominations every week! And every one of those 22,000 denominations has discovered the only "true" interpretation of the Christian faith. Really! Just ask them. They'll tell you. "We're right and everybody else is out to lunch!" As my Jewish friend said, the only thing all the world's religions have in common is that all of them think they are the only ones who are right.

Are all those varieties of spirituality good news or bad news? If you are a flat-footed humanoid like me, it feels like bad news, but maybe if you're God, you are having great fun. Maybe an infinitely imaginative creator God is tickled pink that humans can dream up so many variations on a few basic themes.

And maybe it's only our pea-brained human concepts that keep us from understanding that varieties of contradictory ideas may all contain truth. Or, if you don't like that idea, is it possible that God doesn't care much what we believe, as long as we live with care and integrity?

Durable and Reliable

"The Ten Commandments are derivative," said the learned historian.

This was during a panel discussion on a university campus. The historian pointed out the similarity between those laws and other formulations from earlier times, such as the code of Hammurabi. He was disappointed when I agreed with him. "If it is true that Moses borrowed the Ten Commandments from another culture," I said, "that adds to their credibility, don't you think?"

Every culture has developed some kind of rules or conventions around things like family and sexual relationships, not to mention things like killing and theft. In one sense, there's nothing unique about the Ten Commandments.

Many people find that kind of statement upsetting. I find it reassuring.

I do believe that God communicated to the Hebrew and Christian communities in very unique ways, but that doesn't mean for a moment that God didn't also communicate with others. Hammurabi for instance. Or anyone else who was prepared to listen.

If it could be proved that Moses got those commandments

from Hammurabi, it wouldn't reduce their value one iota. It would mean that God doesn't put all the eggs in one basket and that Moses had the sense to recognize the hand of God in that formulation when he saw it. Inventing truth is God's business. Recognizing it is ours.

Wherever humans try honestly and sincerely to listen, God reaches out to them to offer truth. The truth that God has given to every tribe and nation has been something along these lines: "How you relate to each other is important. You need customs and conventions that honor the needs of the individual and of the community. You need laws that are fair and life-giving. You need a social structure so you don't have to reinvent every relationship."

It doesn't really matter where the particulars came from. The fact is, those Ten Commandments which Moses brought to the Hebrew people thousands of years ago have proven pretty durable and reliable. They are a cage for those who care little for their fellow humans. For those who care about and love God's creation, they offer a foundation for freedom.

The Seven Succulent Sins

The problems of philandering preachers came like a breath of Listermint into the moral climate of North America about a decade ago. Nothing has focused the values of our "post-Christian" nation as effectively as the awareness that we have now added an eighth deadly sin to the traditional seven. It is the most heinous of all.

Getting caught!

Oh, the shame of it all! Tearful TV confessions. And a whole line of products that bring the burden of increased wealth. It is rumored for instance, that Bakker & Swaggart, Inc., will be launching a new magazine called *Repenthouse*, with a centerfold featuring a Praymate. They are also reputed to be jointly authoring a new apologia for TV evangelists called, *Preachers can do more than lay people.*

Let's be grateful to these evangelists. They have helped us focus, once again, on the ancient art of sinning. And just when we thought we had achieved sinlessness through the simple technique of ignoring it or trivializing it.

We have to readjust our thinking, because we hardly know what to do with an ancient concept like sin. My friend Jim Taylor has just authored a fine new book titled *SIN: A new understanding of virtue and vice* which convinces me that all of us can use a good dose of realism and clear thinking about sin. Apparently, it didn't go away – it just went underground like a herpes virus.

Jim Taylor exposes a fundamental irony. All our moralistic little "Thou shalt not's" are as whispers to the advertiser's insistent, "You can have it all!" "You deserve the very best!" "Go for it!" "You're worth it!"

The seven deadly sins, says Jim, have become the seven saving virtues. And since I am always in favor of virtue (who isn't?) I offer this short misinterpretation of Jim's book.

Don't get upset by my cynicism. We need that, when dealing with sin, to flush out the system and dissolve a few layers of perceptual crud before we can deal with reality (which I'll leave up to Jim).

A trivia question. What are the seven deadlies?

Answer: Wrath, Lust, Avarice, Gluttony, Sloth, Envy, Pride.

As a public service, to help reconcile God and Mammon and thus achieve depravity without guilt (our greatest social need), I will help you translate those seven slimy sins into vigorous virtues that are useful, fun, and best of all, profitable.

Lust: Lust is a necessary evil. It's helped us survive centuries of war, death, pestilence and famine, so how can it be called a "deadly" sin? A turn-of-century mother's advice to her daughter approaching the marriage bed was "close your eyes and think of England." Women were expected to sigh in relief when menopause saved them from the necessity of sex. But with the feminist revolution and the pill has come permission for women to lust and enjoy it.

The same permission was given to men, even though most women think the guys enjoyed it all along. We didn't actually. For men, sex is a performance needed to prove to ourselves and others that we are real men. When your pride rises and falls with your penis, it is hard to really enjoy sex, though no red-blooded male would ever admit that. That's why we enjoyed getting older, because we were liberated from our libidos when age took the stuffing out of the old sock.

No longer. Hormone therapy brings back the lust, and we all live happily ever after. More or less.

But be careful of the words you use. We are no longer lusty or horny. No more "loose women" or "dirty old men," but people who are "sexually active."

You may ask, "Is sex no longer dirty?" Well, yes it is. If you do it right.

Pride: It's the "sin you can feel really good about." One of the psalms in the Bible says "Pride goeth before destruction" but not according to my therapist. "Self-confidence is what you need, Ralph." Sports psychologists make a science out of teaching athletes to be "the little engine that could." Any town with a hotel meeting room big enough to hold a few hundred folks finds a steady stream of "self-confidence" gurus parading through preaching the long lost virtue of pride, for a mere five grand a day.

Sloth: You've heard the saying that "necessity is the mother of invention." Forget it. Sloth – good old-fashioned laziness – is the mama. When our forebears got sick of chasing mammoths through the mud they invented agriculture. Several millennia later, when they were too lazy to backpack all the grain around, somebody caught a young bull, nipped off its family jewels, called it an ox, and made it cart the stuff around. The next lazy lummox invented the wheel. The ultimate symbol of sloth is the computer on which I am writing this. Only now we have renamed it "efficiency."

Wrath: With all that sloth around, you need something to wake you up. Well, picture Saddam Hussein and Ralph Nader. Or Margaret Thatcher and Mother Teresa. All of them are angry. The military madman and the antiwar protester are both "wrathed" at something, and that's what makes them do what they do. If we didn't have them, the whole world would sink into terminal torpor. Wrath is the only emotion powerful enough to start a war or to stop one. Only now we call it "commitment."

Envy: A sin? Without this "sin" the commercial world would grind to a halt. The cultivation of envy has become a fine art in the advertising world. We are taught to envy those healthy, active, wide awake, popular, motivated, wonderful young party goers in the beer ads. The solution to our envy is to drink beer, even though anyone who thinks for a moment, knows that beer brings a bulging "Molson muscle" and turns us into couch potatoes. But envy, when done properly, doesn't allow for thinking. And please don't call it envy. Call it "ambition" or "goal setting." Sometimes envy goes under the name of "financial planning."

Avarice: Okay, let's make it simple. Call it greed. Who is the living symbol? The patron saint of greed is Santa. Who else? Every year, we give our kids lessons in the articulation of greed. We get them to write letters to Santa. We have even set aside a special day to celebrate this noble passion. We call it Christmas. And if merchandisers have their way, we'll turn Easter and Valentines Day, hell, every day into Christmas. Like all the other succulent seven, this sin needs a new name. "You deserve the very best," says the ad, so why not simply call it "fulfillment."

Gluttony: Gluttony is the most socially acceptable of all sins/virtues. For the finest modern theoretical expression of this art, look at the food magazines near the check-out stands in the supermarkets. For its quintessential practical expression, look to the cruise ships plying our waters, where the whales in the ocean are only slightly slimmer than the whales onboard. But gluttony sounds awful, so let's call it "nutrition."

Our forebears tried to eliminate sin by encouraging people to be more moral, but that never worked very well. Now our generation has taken the next logical and efficient step by rationalizing sin and renaming it.

The socially conscious and liberal leaning among us – Christian or otherwise – have eliminated personal sin as a matter of concern in favor of corporate sin. Corporate sin is much more fun to rail at, because it's always "them" and never "us." Getting caught at personal sin is not an issue for the left, because it has named personal sin as a repressive concept promoted by an oppressive hierarchical structure. Those on the left put on their Birkenstocks, get into their Volvos, and drive to retreat centers where they eat organically grown vegetarian dishes and complain about multi-nationals. They are allowed to do anything they want as long as they wear the right lapel buttons and T-shirts.

Right-wing conservative types and evangelicals have simply baptized the seven deadly sins and called them "the American Way." You can justify anything you do if you do it in the name of Jesus or the flag. Just don't get caught with your *lederhosen* around your legs. And don't forget to turn whatever you do into a virtue, a mission – like downsizing the national deficit by cutting back on child support payments to single moms. (For their own good, and the good of the country, of course.)

For the left: "Anything's okay as long as it's liberating."

For the right: "Anything's okay as long as it stimulates the economy or you pray about it first.

Cynical?

Well, yes. Just a tad. We need cynicism to act like a good shot of WD-40 (a rust-dissolving lubricant) because there is almost nothing that seizes up our moral mechanism like our amazing ability to talk ourselves out of our own sin. My cynicism, I hope, will get you reading Jim's book and doing some serious thinking about sin.

Because those seven deadly sins, when we turn them into the seven saving virtues, will eat us up. From the inside out.

Why People Quit

At our office, we get lots of motivational materials designed to make our company more profitable and to make our marketing efforts more effective. Recently we got sent some research which the folks in sales read with interest.

It asked the question, "Why do customers leave us and go buy somewhere else? Then it answered its own question.

1% die
3% move away
5% other friendships
9% competitive reasons (price)
14% product dissatisfaction. But...
68% quit because of an attitude of indifference
toward them by some employee!!

That got me wondering about service clubs and churches and other volunteer organizations. Why do some people leave for no apparent reason? Why do some people come once or twice and then disappear?

Last week I went to a service club in Vancouver. I was on the "rubber-chicken circuit" again, making speeches at the request of program chairpersons who have to fill up half an hour with someone, anyone, who can talk that long without stopping.

I arrived 15 minutes early. The program chair said "welcome," got me a cup of coffee, and disappeared. I stood there feeling conspicuous while the folks talked to each other in little groups. Then the chairperson came and sat me down at the head table. There were polite introductions. The meal was served.

The man on my right talked to the man on his right. The man on my left talked to the man on his left. Nobody talked to me. The club president stood up and complained about the falling membership and that people didn't attend very faithfully anymore. Not like the good old days. Then I made my speech, took my fee, and we all went home.

It's funny. I didn't have an overwhelming urge to join.

Mutual Support

We visited the giant redwoods on a trip to California recently. These magnificent giants stand as much as 300 feet tall and are hundreds of years old. How do they survive that long? How come the strong winds blowing off the Pacific ocean don't topple them?

A signboard in a park provided the answer. Giant Redwoods seldom grow alone. Their shallow root systems spread out and intertwine with the roots of the other giant redwoods, and in that way they support each other.

That's why giant redwoods always grow in clusters. They need each other for mutual support.

Cranky Christmas

If you go to church regularly, this joke will strike you as painfully funny.

The couple were driving past the church. It was late December. The snow was falling on a lovely crèche – Mary, Joseph, baby Jesus, sheep, shepherds, wise men – the works. "Look at that," he says to her. "Even the churches are trying to horn in on Christmas."

If you're *not* a church goer, it will seem like a reasonable grump. Why should the churches take a perfectly good bash and try to make something religious out of it?

But you see, Christmas is a Christian celebration, and Christian folks get a bit testy when the commercial mandarins take it away from them. That's why they cry while they laugh at that joke.

The church didn't start Christmas because December 25th was the day Jesus was born. Nobody *knows* when Jesus was born.

It certainly wasn't on December 25th because there are no "shepherds abiding in the fields keeping watch over their flock by night" in Israel at the end of December. The weather's too cold and miserable. We don't even know what *year* Jesus was born.

Christmas got started a few centuries after the time of Jesus, when the church was well-established, but the folks in Rome were still having an annual bash called *Sol Invictus*, or the Festival of the Invincible Sun. The Romans held it when the days started getting a bit longer, after the winter solstice. The early Christians began celebrating the birth of Christ at the same time, just so they'd have something to be joyful about while the rest of the Roman world was having a big booze-up. When Christianity became the official religion, they renamed *Sol Invictus* "Christ Mass," which has been shortened to Christmas.

In the last 50 years or so, Christmas has turned into a big spending and boozing bash, and some of us are wondering if we should just return to the old Roman celebration. The secularization of Christmas creates problems for those who would still like it to be a festival to commemorate the birth of Christ. It's a losing battle, because when folks start getting cabin fever during those long winter nights, especially here in Canada, they love nothing better than to head for the malls where the fluorescents burn brightly till nine or ten every night. Whatever the reasons, the focus of Christmas has been moved from the church to the shopping center.

It's not that us good church folk don't like Christmas. We love it. The churches are packed to the gunwales with hyper kids and strung-out adults trying to capture the "spirit of Christmas," which is really more nostalgia than spirituality. People flock to church, wanting to hear the old story and sing the old carols. When the adult kids come home for Christmas, mama drags all of them to the Singing Christmas Tree, or the Christmas Eve service or Midnight Mass. Even the Jewish community gets in on the act by fluffing up the minor festival of *Chanukah* so they'll have something to do while all their Christian neighbors are whooping it up.

Still, there's one thing we *all* agree on. Every one of us – Catholics, Protestants, even Jews. We belly-ache about the terrible commercialization of Christmas! "Ain't it awful," we sob all the way to and from the malls.

I am told that the folks at Sears and Spiegal gather each Boxing Day to look over the sales figures and sing a chorus or two of "What a friend we have in Jesus." And the folks at Eaton's join in, even though old Timothy who founded Eaton's was a good, Jesus-believing Methodist and must be doing flip-flops in his grave.

I'm sorry.

I find it so easy to be cynical about Christmas. It's particularly bad for me in mid-December when I can hardly walk through one of the malls without throwing up. Its the schmaltzy "elevator music" versions of Christmas hymns on the PA systems – *O Come All Ye Faithful, Silent Night* – that make me gag. That's when I want to say, "Give it to 'em. If Sears and Spiegel and Eaton's and Henry's Underwear Emporium want Christmas, let 'em have it."

But anybody can take cheap shots at Christmas! I find it hard to keep my cynicism from outrunning my good sense. Nobody wants to hear from a Christmas crank.

At such times, I find it best to talk to someone who hasn't had their spirit contaminated by as many years. I talk to Zoë.

Zoë will be a year and a few weeks old this Christmas, and she knows more about these things than I do. She was the baby Jesus in the Christmas pageant last year at her church. Her nervous mom got to be Mary and her anxious dad was Joseph. Grandpa got to sit in a pew and cry like an old fool.

Zoë hasn't forgotten what it was like to be Jesus – the child of hope. Her life is built on hope. Not some mushy Pollyanna optimism, but a built-in sense that life is to be lived for all it's worth and full-tilt. Zoë has just learned to crawl, but she only has one speed – as fast as she can make her small legs go. And she drinks in new life with relish and with joy, and cries and laughs as the spirit moves her.

Maybe when I tell her how steamed up I get about phony Christmas consumerism she'll let me know how Jesus would feel.

After I explain all my frustration, she may just give my beard a tug. That will be her way of telling me that feeling Grandpa's bristly beard and seeing what he does when you pull it, is far more fundamentally important than all his mental wrestlings. When Zoë tugs my beard, the Christ child tugs my beard and tells me that in each new birth God invests the hope of the world.

"Put a sock in it!" I'll tell the old cynic in my head. Then I'll hold my granddaughter close and feel the power of her newborn love.

And Zoë on her second Christmas and me on my 62nd will celebrate the festival of Hope together.

How to Make a Jesus Movie

I have decided to fulfill my life-long ambition, and make a movie about the life of Jesus. It is going to be a billion-dollar spectacular.

It will be a family movie, of course, so the first scene will be Mary and Joseph on the road to Bethlehem. Good movies about Jesus, at least the kind that sell, always start there because that's the sentimental part. Babies being born are always good for openers.

I will need a budget for research. The first thing is to find out exactly what kind of donkey Mary used so she could ride in her long, pale blue dress.

That's easier said than done, because the Bible doesn't say anything about a donkey at all. It just says they "went" to Bethlehem. It doesn't say anything about a long, pale blue dress either, but everybody knows that's what Mary wore so she wouldn't look too pregnant on all the Christmas cards.

Then I'll need a budget to build the manger set. We've seen it a zillion times on the lawns at the shopping centers. Mary in a clean blue gown looking as if she just stepped out of a shower, and Joseph pleased as punch. And there's shepherds and wise guys and a brilliant spotlight shining down on a healthy, sleek cow and several woolly sheep. And the baby Jesus is kicking the air with fat cuddly feet.

Everybody expects the Christmas card manger. And this is the entertainment business, after all. It's the bottom line that's important. You have to give people what they want and expect.

I just wish I could get out of my head a trip to Israel several years ago where I saw a Bedouin stable. My guide was an expert on the Bible. He said, "That's probably pretty close to the kind of stable Jesus was born in."

It was filthy. Utterly filthy.

The animals were skinny and flee bitten, with sores all over them. And the place was full of rats and cockroaches.

And it stank. It stank so bad, even my farm-boy eyes watered.

But I can't put *that* kind of a stable in my Jesus movie. It's got to be a sweet, clean stable with bare-bottomed cherubs singing on the roof.

If I showed Jesus born in a stinking, rotten, cockroach infested barn like the kind I saw in Israel, that would say he came into the world in the same painful, dirty way he left it. That's not what people want. That starts to feel like some kind of reli-

gious statement about Jesus identifying with the poor folks –
the hurting folks. But this is a family movie so we have to keep
religion out of it.

Which brings me to another problem. I've read all four versions of the story of Jesus in the Bible and none of them have
enough action to make a good movie script. Jesus mostly walks
around the countryside talking to people. I kept looking for the
scene where he'd really take it to the bad guys, all those Scribes
and Pharisees and Romans in black hats, and wipe them out.
Isn't there a good Jewish karate or kung-fu of some kind that he
might have used? Couldn't he have raised an army so we could
have some gory battle scenes with heads getting chopped off and
blood gushing out. You need that if you want it to be a family
movie that'll keep the kids interested.

There's some good blood and gore in the crucifixion scene,
but it sure would be nice if Jesus fought back a little. One of the
other guys on the cross beside him gives him a good line. "C'mon
Jesus," he says, "get down off that cross. Save yourself and me
too." But all Jesus does is forgive everyone. No real action at all.

The resurrection stuff has some potential, but it really needs
a scene where Jesus busts out of the grave with a huge explosion
and takes the Scribes and Pharisees and Romans and all the rest
of the bad guys by surprise and wipes them all out.

Except he doesn't do that. The resurrected Jesus seems to spend
his time talking to people and telling them how to catch fish.

That's why the budget for this movie is so high. When you
have a wimpy script to start with, you need to bring in the re-
write folks to goose it up – a few good lines. A bunch of action.
Special effects.

Like at the end of that dinner party, you could have Jesus
saying, "Okay, Judas. Make my day."

Then we'd cut to the Garden of Gethsemane where Jesus and Peter and the boys would wipe out the guard that comes to arrest them. Jesus would put his arm around a voluptuous Mary of Magdala to save her from being violated by a centurion who has torn her dress almost off. Jesus would vault onto a white horse and whisk Mary off into the hills where the two of them would have a good, passionate love scene. Then Jesus would train a troop of crack guerrilla fighters who blow up the aqueducts and finally liberate the country from the Romans and the Scribes and Pharisees and all the rest of the bad guys.

You see, a film about Jesus should be a happy movie with a good positive message – the good guys always beat the bad guys in the end. That gives everyone a nice warm feeling.

And we'd release it just in time for the holiday season so that people can get the true meaning of Christmas.

Holy Pantyhose!

A friend told us once about a radio advertisement for "genuine imitation diamond rings," which was followed by an ad selling "autographed pictures of Jesus Christ that glow in the dark."

We thought he was kidding until *The Wittenberg Door* (a kind of evangelical *Mad Magazine*) reproduced an ad for an "LED Cross." Not only does the image of Jesus light up, but a "message of inspiration" and a "pulsating heart" appear. Such benefits! "Never feel alone again. Gently touch your cross and our Lord will lovingly appear with His message just for you."

If that doesn't satisfy your cynical heart, how about some "Gold Cross Fragrant Pantyhose?" There's a gold cross on every pair, just about half-way up the calf. "Every Christian woman should wear them," presumably to evangelize the lechers.

Such imaginative evangelistic efforts are to be applauded. We are told there's another type of pantyhose available with John 3:16 printed up near the thigh. In Braille.

That's probably a bit more practical than the guy who goes to major sporting events and finds the seat right where the camera will be pointed most often. Then he flashes a sign that says "John 3:16." Do viewers know what John 3:16 is? If they already know it, do they need to be reminded? If they don't know what it is, will they look it up? The answers to the above can be found on page 793 of this book.

Ian Macdonald, a friend of mine with a wonderful imagination, once proposed that a great form of evangelism would be to release 800,000 gerbils with John 3:16 spray-painted on their backs during the Grey Cup football championship. That would certainly generate some ecstatic utterances!

Macdonald was kidding, of course. The others weren't, unfortunately. Neither were the misguided folks who proposed a compromise in the battle over whether to install condom dispensing machines in high schools. The condoms were to have Bible verses printed on them.

Those folks really understood the nature of young love. Or lust. But they didn't explain who would do the reading, and whether you read the Bible verse before, after, or during.

All of which proves nothing, except that people's zeal sometimes outruns their good sense.

When the Ordinary Becomes Holy

The 39 folk in our rag-tag band of travelers came from many sorts of backgrounds. Some had spiritual roots. Others didn't.

We were traveling through Europe – just another group of miscellaneous people on a tour bus.

But a community began to grow, as we learned to move and laugh and sometimes cry together. By the time we started north out of Italy, a few of the younger people in the group began to feel that we should celebrate our community with a communion service. A straw poll showed that others shared their view.

Our "atheist" bus driver and "agnostic" tour director knocked themselves out to find just the right place for this event, a remote and glorious viewpoint near the Italian-Swiss border where range after range of mountains offered glimpses of eternity. Surely this was the most beautiful spot on earth – a place where we could see forever.

And so we gathered there surrounded by magnificence. We heard, we reflected on words almost as old as those mountains. "When I consider the work of thy hands, the moon and the stars, who are we, that You are mindful of us?"

Then, a borrowed kerchief became a cloth for our table. A borrowed mug became a chalice. A borrowed scarf became a stole for Bev, our priest. A piece of rock became an altar. The common wine and ordinary bread were sanctified by our community and by an eternity of mountains and an infinity of sky.

On that mountainside, our little straggly band of wanderers remembered and renewed a covenant made centuries before, at another table-rock altar, by another band of wanderers led by Abraham and Sarah.

We reached backward in history and forward in time and wondered out loud at the miracle – how God takes ordinary things and makes them holy. An ordinary rock becomes an altar; cheap wine and corner-store bread become the gift of life.

A bus load of tourists become heirs to the Promise.

And for that little moment, our tiny band of stragglers was a church.

The Whole World in God's Hands

Honky in My Blood

"Be the best damned honky you know how to be," said Harrison. "Don't even try to pretend you are a 'brother'."

We were at a community potluck supper, and I was asking Harrison how to make the chitlins he had brought. He told me I couldn't. "You got the wrong color skin," he said. "You stick to that brown pudding." He was referring to the Mennonite *pluma mouse* I had brought.

Harrison lived next door to us in Teaneck, New Jersey. He had moved there from the Bronx, and was a radical in the Black Liberation movement during the '6os.

I was doing time as a bureaucrat in a Manhattan office tower that looked like an orange crate on end. We lived in the "burbs" and I commuted through the traffic and the smog across the George Washington bridge every day.

Our particular "burb" had been a nice, middle-class, liberal, "wasp" suburb that was rapidly turning over to African Americans from the Bronx and Jewish people from the Brooklyn. We had moved into a district where all our children's friends were African American or Jewish. We were the only "honkies" in the neighborhood.

Naturally, we tried to adapt. Naturally, we failed miserably. In the process we found some fine friends. "You got 'honky' in your blood," said Harrison. "That's okay. Just don't play games and I'll love you for it!"

The conversations with Harrison were not always comfortable. Sometimes I'd get my consciousness abruptly jacked up a notch or two.

"What's this 'black and white issue' eh? Black is bad? White is good?"

"I didn't mean that."

"No, but you said it. Clean up your language."

Harrison was an angry young man and not easy to talk to. But I always learned a little.

Through our daughter, we became good friends with Fran and Jack Levine who were faithfully observant Jews. They walked to synagogue every Sabbath and observed all the dietary laws. As our friendship grew, we began a tradition of inviting each other for our high holy days.

"Don't wash it clean with Christian Lysol," said Fran when we invited the Levines over for Christmas dinner. So we sang *Away in a manger* and *Silent Night* and read the whole Christmas story from the Bible. And we prayed in the name of "Our Lord and Savior Jesus Christ." Fran wanted it "straight up" so that's how we served it.

We knew that was okay, because when we had joined them for Passover they became elaborately Jewish. "So are you maybe Moses?" asked Fran. "Because how come suddenly I'm such a Yiddishe Mama?"

Our family was wonderfully enriched by the Levines who shared their traditions with us. And by allowing us to share our traditions with them, we understood, as old Tevya says in *Fiddler on the Roof*, "who we are and what God expects us to do."

And Fran made the most wonderful *blintse*.

I don't think we're called to be people in general, but a person in particular.

Not a person in isolation, though. I live in a community that extends outward in space and backward in time. I am a person with roots, with heritage, with a particular set of stories and metaphors and legends and traditions through which I express who I am.

One of the prairie traditions I grew up with is the potluck supper. The best kind are when people bring favorite dishes out of their own ethnic heritage. Every dish is enjoyed and appreciated because it is individual and unique. Everybody collects compliments on their particular dish.

I make *pluma mouse* which literally means "plum soup," even though it does look sort of brown and nondescript, as Harrison noticed. It's half pudding, half soup, but in my Mennonite tradition it is eaten as a main course. It is also very easy to make and almost impossible to ruin, which is why I make it often. I usually put the recipe beside it, with my name on it so I can collect the compliments while I am enjoying everyone else's food.

Pluma mouse is one tiny sliver of a sacred trust – a trust that impels me to share the gifts I have, to express the personality I have been given, to sing the songs I know, to tell the stories I was raised on, to be who I am.

All of it.

Joyfully.

And to share that as faithfully and as warmly as I can while I open myself to Harrison and to Fran and to all the rest of this wonderful and diverse creation.

In God's great potluck supper world, don't dump everything into one pot. Savor each individual dish. Enjoy its uniqueness.

And talk to its Creator.

One Size Fits All

In men's clothing stores there's sometimes a sign over the sock rack that says, "one size fits all." Except that one size doesn't fit me nor my friend Aaron who has very small feet.

"One size fits all" is an idea that doesn't work for language either. Especially for language about God.

I am a wordsmith by trade. I use words the way carpenters use planks and boards and nails and screws, often to build things that are necessary and simply utilitarian, but sometimes to fashion something beautiful. Because I write a lot about values and spirituality and relationships, most of the building materials I use are metaphors.

A metaphor is a way of talking about something when you really have no adequate way of talking about it. For instance, there is no way I can describe the beauty, talents, intelligence and sheer wonder I see in Zoë and Jake, my grandkids. I could bore you out of your ever-lovin' mind bragging about them, but I am more likely to show you some snapshots.

"See what wonderful, beautiful, intelligent grandkids I have?"

"Ahh, they look like, ah, normal children to me."

"C'mon. Take a look at their faces. These kids are geniuses!"

"Sure, yeah. I'm sure they must be. You can't really tell from a photo, can you? But hey, I'm sorry! Gotta run."

No photo will ever do justice to Jake and Zoë. Or to anybody else for that matter. A photo is like a metaphor. It's inadequate, but the best we can do, short of meeting the subject in person. And it's a little pointless arguing about how much the photo shows or doesn't show.

We get ourselves into the glue over and over because we think of metaphors as fact, when they are actually just a flying approximation – a glimpse of an idea. Because metaphors are the only way we can talk about the deepest realities of life, we treat them as if they are objective truth.

There's a lively argument going on in many religious circles, from far out New Age groupies to tradition bound conservatives, about how to talk about God. You can get some dandy arguments going about whether one should be "politically correct" about God, or whether God is male or female, etc., etc., *ad nauseam.*

Eco-feminists speak of Gaia, originally a Greek earth goddess, as the divine force that brings all of creation together as a unified organism. At the other end of the religious spectrum, we find the dogged insistence that God is male and that "Father" is the only appropriate word to describe "Him."

Gaia and Father are both metaphors. Like snapshots, metaphors show things that words cannot express. But they don't show everything. In fact, some metaphors, especially metaphors for God, hide more than they reveal. No metaphor, no snapshot, ever does the whole job. They always leave something important out. They often include something that distorts the picture.

On the other hand, all metaphors about God are right in some ways. All of them show us a glimpse of one aspect of that indescribable something that is God. So all metaphors are both right and wrong. In *God for Beginners,* I offered ten unusual metaphors for God, everything from "rock star" to "computer hack." All of them had some aspect of truth. None of them was completely adequate. Most of them would be offensive to somebody.

Some people have tried to solve the problem of what to call God by becoming as clinical and detached as possible. They sometimes use terms like "life force" or "creative energy," but those are metaphors too, although very weak ones. They're a bit like showing you snapshots of my grandkids with the faces cut out.

"Well, I don't want to force my concept of grandchildren on you. I just want to celebrate generic grandchildren, not any grandchildren in particular. So I cut their faces out." That generic grandchild concept might not offend anyone, but it won't inspire anyone either. Pictures of faceless grandchildren are boring. A generic, no-name God is even less interesting.

All-purpose, politically correct metaphors often backfire. They may be totally inclusive, but they are so broad and clinical and detached that nobody feels particularly inspired. It's hard to develop a relationship with a "primal energy," or even the more traditional "prime mover."

I propose the Sprat solution:

Jack Sprat could eat no fat,
His wife could eat no lean.
And so between the both of them,
They licked the platter clean.

If the Sprats had followed our usual practices of inclusiveness as we apply it to language, they'd both have starved to death. But they found a better way. Jack ate lean. Jill ate fat. If they'd followed the usual rules of inclusive language, they would both have to eat everything or nothing and both starve or get indigestion.

They used a better and even more inclusive principle. Not *everything* for everybody, but *something* for everyone. "You eat the lean," says Jill. "I'll eat the fat." Between the two of them, they cleaned up the platter, patted their tummies and belched. Both were satisfied, but neither said, "Because you didn't eat what I ate, I feel excluded and marginalized."

Bev, at the moment, is on a restricted diet. She's not supposed to eat animal fats because of her high cholesterol, and she's got to stay away from sugar because of her triglycerides. So when we go out to eat, we go where there is a big smorg. She can find what she wants and needs and I can find what I want and need. She does not demand that the high-fat, high-sugar stuff be removed from the smorg. She just wants there to be choices for everyone.

My doctor mentioned to me once that every medication, every treatment, has negative side effects for some people. The doctor weighs the risks of using the medication versus the risk of not using it. There are risks either way. Penicillin has saved millions of lives. It has also killed some people who have had reactions. In every treatment that heals, yes, *every* treatment, there is the risk of severe negative effects. Even if you do nothing, you risk negative side effects.

The language we use can and should be an instrument of healing. The most healing language is that which touches the soul – that moves the spirit. That kind of language is always made up of risky images, and dangerous, loaded metaphors – the very things that will be most painful to those with deep wounds. Language that is healing for many will always have bad side effects for some. There is no right word, no correct metaphor for God.

Thinking of God as mother works for me because I had a loving and caring mom, but I have a friend whose mother abused and abandoned her. She was raised by a loving uncle. For her, that's a good metaphor for God. So she can relate to God as her Uncle, and I can relate to God as my Mother, and you can call God whatever works for you.

Hundreds of years ago, a medieval monk wrote a little book called *A Thousand Names for God*. He had the right idea. Let's use lots of different metaphors so that along the way each of us finds one we can really relate to. If we try to find one that fits everyone, we'll all be left out.

As the old wag said, "I don't care what you call me as long as you don't call me late for supper." I don't think God cares either what name we use. But I *do* think God cares that we call.

"One size fits all," says the sign on the sock rack.

Horse apples! My feet are too big and my toe sticks through those socks the second time I wear them; Aaron's feet are too small and the socks bunch up at the toes of his shoes.

"One size fits all," doesn't work for language either.

Y'all Soak Your Heads

"What do you guys want for dessert?" she asked. "Ooops, I forgot. The boss says I'm not supposed to say 'you guys' anymore. What do you folks want for dessert?"

"'Folks' makes us sound like dottering octogenarians," he said.

"All right. So what would you 'people' like for dessert?" she asked through partially clenched teeth.

"'People' is too impersonal. Too detached."

"Humankind?"

"Likewise too detached. Impersonal."

"Friends," she smiled as best she could. "What would my dear friends like for dessert?"

"Too intimate," he said dully. "You hardly know us."

"Idiots," she yelled. "What do you idiots want for dessert?"

"Judgmental," he said.

"I give up. You come up with a usable alternative, or there's no dessert."

"Y'all."

"Huh?"

"Y'all," he said. A good non-sexist term for a group of people. We can import it from the deep south. What could be more inclusive than 'Y'all'?"

"Y'all go and soak your head," she said. "Y'hear?"

Prejudice and Pizza

On the bulletin board at St. Paul's Seminary in Ottawa I notice something – a menu from a local pizza takeout place.

First, I am surprised to see a menu from a pizzeria on the bulletin board at a Catholic seminary.

Then I am surprised at being surprised.

I am surprised because, even though I have had deep, intense and extensive involvement with Catholics of all stripes and colors, and know them to have all the virtues and vices that the rest of us have, I have the soul of a small-town Mennonite boy who thinks Catholic priests wear black suits and white collars and spend all their time praying incomprehensible Latin.

It makes no sense. I have worked and lived with priests – lots of them – and I count a number of them as good friends. That's why I am so surprised at being surprised. Does some of my mother's anti-Catholicism still infect me?

It's not the first time I've been blind-sided by my own racism or sexism or homophobia or ageism or anti-Semitism or whatever. I'm infected by all of those, so I might as well admit that right off the top. I think of myself as the essence of informed liberalism and I should have exorcised all those demons years ago. But I haven't. I'm sorry. "I have left undone those things I ought to have done and I have done those things I ought not to have done, and my mind is all messed up," to paraphrase St. Paul who had similar frustrations.

My first awareness of this problem came in 1961 after we arrived in the Philippines. Bev and I were watching the Independence Day parade, made up mostly of students from the university where were lived – students who had to enroll in the military auxiliary as part of their studies. They marched past us in lock step, rifles on shoulders, eyes straight ahead. Bev and I stood on the sidelines, and all of a sudden we became aware that we were squeezing each other's hands in fear. Deep, visceral fear.

We no longer saw Juan and Pedro and Ernesto and Dodung, our friends whom we knew by name, who often came to our home and ate our peanut butter sandwiches. Suddenly we felt the fear drilled into us as children during World War II – images of the maniacal Japanese hordes with buck teeth and slant eyes – madmen out to destroy civilization whom we saw depicted in the propaganda comic books and the war movies. Our adult minds no longer believed those lies, but the fear lived on in our childhood memories, and now it surfaced when we saw these brown-skinned soldiers marching in lock step before us.

This made no sense! We knew those young men. They were our friends. And the Philippines had suffered more than almost any other country from the Japanese invasion. Most of all it made no sense because Bev and I had long ago rejected racist concepts and ideas. But there were those feelings – misdirected and illogical, but real. Far too real.

I have a friend who grew up in southern Texas. Gene absorbed the racism of his culture, the hatred of "wetbacks" and "niggers!" But he rejected that racism firmly when he entered university, and even more when he entered the Methodist ministry. But Gene was also aware that those attitudes are not purged by a simple intellectual decision, so he went to Africa and spent his life there, and among other things, worked to rid himself of his racism. He was married by this time to a fine woman who shared his convictions. Together they raised a family in Africa.

Let Gene tell the rest of the story. "When Adele, my eldest daughter was ready for university, we sent her off to the States. About a year later when I was in Texas for a visit, she phoned me and we arranged to meet on her campus. 'There's someone I want you to meet,' she said, and I could tell from her voice she was in love. Well, I saw them coming across the campus toward me, hand in hand, and all my insides did a flip-flop. The man was black. I found myself raging angry. The thought occurred to me that maybe he had been in bed with her, and then I wanted only to kill him, with my bare hands if possible. At the same time, my mind yelled at me, 'This makes no sense Gene. Your daughter grew up in Africa. All her childhood friends were African. It's only normal that she would relate to an African American.' But I couldn't quell the rage that boiled inside me. Rage at myself, too, because I had worked all my life to get rid of my racism, and there it was, as virulent as ever."

The good news is that Gene managed to be civil to the young man until his rage subsided, and eventually he was able to confess his feelings and talk them through. "It worked out just fine in the end," said Gene, "but it was certainly a learning experience." Then he added sadly, "I guess I'll go to my grave with my racism."

So will I. Racism is a bit like alcoholism, I suppose. They tell me that an alcoholic is always an alcoholic, but that the alcoholic can choose not to drink. I am racist, sexist, homophobic, ageist,

166 • Angels in Red Suspenders

anti-Semitic and a few other awful things I don't even have names for. I don't want to be, but I am. So my only choice is to consciously act as I believe, and not let those cultural demons control me. I can't always choose how I will feel, but I can choose how I will act. Gradually my living will drive those ghosts into hiding, but probably not extinction. And I should not be surprised when they surprise me.

But pizza eating priests! What do you call that? Anti-clerical-pizzaism? The appropriate treatment, I think, is to phone a couple of my priest friends and get them to order in some pizza and open a large bottle of Chianti, and then they can counsel me.

Especially if they pick up the tab.

The Color of Your Skin

"Red and yellow, black and white..." We sing that old song without thinking how silly it is. It's like a line Rudyard Kipling might have written. Kipling, who wrote of "lesser breeds without the law" and "the white man's burden," might have written that ridiculous line in that very familiar children's hymn, "Jesus loves the little children, all the children of the world..."

I've seen and known many aboriginal North Americans, but never seen one that was red. I lived in Asia for five years but never saw anyone who was yellow.

I lived in New Jersey, in a neighborhood where we were the only "white" family during the time it became acceptable to use the term "black" to replace the previously acceptable "Negro." Both terms of course referred to African Americans. But I never saw a black person in the US, though I did see some in Africa that were very close. A beautiful, deep ebony.

I've never seen a white person for that matter, even though Kipling would have said I was one of those "white men" with the "burden." I'm a desk jockey. My skin is light brown.

My colleague Jim Taylor fussed over the line from the children's song and came up with a good alternative. "Short and tall and dark and light." It's got the right number of syllables and it rhymes. What's more, it's far more inclusive. Especially in the color category because people really do come in a delightful variety of pigmentations.

It's astounding the agony and social struggle we go through over such a minor genetic difference as the color of our skin. Yet in almost every society, skin color has enormous social and political implications.

Years ago, when we lived in the Philippines, we used to chuckle whenever we went down to the local beach. We lived on the Silliman University campus and there were always a dozen or so American exchange students studying there.

The Americans students and their Filipino friends would head down to the beach on weekends, as students seem to do everywhere. The Caucasian Americans would lie out in the sun, baking their backsides unmercifully so they could go back home with a status tan. Their Filipino friends huddled under the nearest tree or umbrella trying desperately to keep the sun off of their already tan skins. For them, the paler the skin, the higher the status. The only ones indifferent to this ritual were the African American students who told me, "we can get sunburned, all right. It hurts, but it doesn't show."

Skin color is a sign of wealth. Or lack of it.

In the Philippines, poor people work out in the fields or live in the streets in the hot tropical sun and develop a dark skin. Only the well-to-do can afford to be indoors and stay pale. In

North America, poor people work indoors and live in apartments. Only the wealthy can afford to bask in the sun so a tan is a sign of wealth.

Skin color or condition is also a sign of status. Or lack of it.

Any drugstore displays rack after rack of lotions and potions to keep your skin soft and free of wrinkles or pimples or any other "disfiguration."

On my hands, I can see an increasing number of brown blotches. They're called liver spots, and they happen to folks as they get older. There is really nothing you can do about them. Nor should you.

On my face, wrinkles. Skin color changes with age. Skin texture too.

I stand up to the mirror with Zoë, her face next to mine. We look at ourselves together. Her face is soft and smooth and wonderful to touch. Mine is wrinkled and blotched and bearded. I like Zoë's one-year-old face. She snuggles up to me and gives my beard a tug. I think she likes my 62-year-old face.

Zoë and I have something the drugstores don't sell. Enlightenment, as the Buddhists might call it, or grace, to use a Christian term.

It comes when we look in the mirror, see our skin and say, "Yes, that's exactly the way it should be."

Looking Past the Fear

Dad was fluently trilingual. He spoke English, German, and the "low-German" of the Russian Mennonites.

So during World War II, Dad worked with the censorship department of the armed forces, checking mail between a group of German prisoners incarcerated in Canada and their families in Europe.

The job wasn't all that hard. The pay was good. During the three years he did the job, Dad didn't find a thing in any of the mail that could be called "sensitive information." But he did begin to see the war through different eyes.

During the war, Germans and Japanese were portrayed in the North American media as power-mad maniacs out to conquer the world and destroy civilization. But Dad couldn't find those kinds of Germans in the mail he was reading. "They're ordinary people, just like us, and they are just as confused and upset about what is going on as we are."

Dad was technically in the military. He could have been court-marshaled for some of the things he told us kids. He could have been thrown in the slammer for bringing home some beautifully etched artwork a mother had sent to Hans, her son in prison. All artwork was suspect and to be destroyed, said the rules, but Dad slipped it in his pocket and brought it home to show us.

It was exquisite and tender. It showed a broken stump and at its base was a sapling. The words beneath it said, "That stump is our beloved father. You are the sapling." It was a notice of his father's death that my dad could not send on to Hans.

After the war, Dad located Hans in Germany. His mother had disappeared in the war. Hans had no other mementos of his family.

Dad helped me see through different eyes. As a boy, I learned that in any conflict good is never only on one side. Nor evil. Dad looked past the caricature of fear and saw in the "enemy" a child of God.

While Standing at a Cenotaph

I heard two 12-year-old boys discussing a video they'd just seen.

"Did you see how he sliced this guy's belly open and the guts just peeled out?"

"Yeah," said the other boy. "It was cool when you saw his whole brain explode. Bam. Blood all over everything."

H.L. Mencken once observed that "war will never cease until babies come into the world with larger cerebrums and smaller adrenal glands."

That's no doubt true but it's not very likely. Recent studies seem to show that males, particularly, are victims of their own testosterone, the male hormone. Some scientists say males are hard-wired to be aggressive and combative. If that is true, lads, we may be an endangered species. Women have always suspected they could get on quite nicely without us, and unless we can stop acting like orangutans in heat, they may decide that cloning the best of them is better than putting up with the worst of us.

When I was nine years old, I got into a great fight with Jimmy Bennett in the school yard. Our scrap was cheered on by a small circle of supporters who enjoyed watching us bloody each other's noses. The principal came out, grabbed us both by the scruff of our necks, hauled us into his office, and said, "I don't know what you two are fighting about, but I want you to shake hands, apologize to each other, and be friends from now on. That's an order."

So we did and we were. Best buds for years.

Not all human conflicts are resolved that neatly, but that principal knew something. You stop the wars, you stop the killing, by taking direct action right where you live.

For instance, it's sometimes argued that the gratuitous carnage we see on TV and on videos – that violence in sports and war-toys for children – is a harmless diversion – a helpful release for normal energy. Horse feathers!

There's no end of research that shows conclusively that media violence feeds the killer instinct in us. War, rape, street killings and domestic murder begin in the family rooms of our own respectable suburban homes. And we males, who turn out really to be "the weaker sex," are the most vulnerable to this evil stimulus.

We can sing songs and march in parades, but we really honor the men and women who died in wars while fighting for peace, only if we continue to work for peace in our own homes. If all we do is make pious noises and do nothing to stop the evil against which they fought – nothing to promote the peace for which they died – then we make a mockery of their sacrifice. It would be better to stay home, then to go out to that cenotaph and be hypocritical.

International treaties and other big stuff are not really that important. It's the small stuff at home that counts. The struggle for peace begins where we live and with a fundamental recognition – the violence on TV, the gore on rental videos, the war toys we buy, are training our boy babies to be killers.

Simplistic Solutions

"Look at the sawfly in there," said Don.

I looked. I didn't see any sawfly.

"Well, you don't actually see the sawfly," said Don, "but you see how some of the stalks are cut off. That's the sawfly grub."

I took another look. All I saw was a grain field. I wasn't even sure what kind of grain it was. I thought it must be barley, remembering back 40 years to my uncle's farm in southern

Manitoba. "Nope," said Don. "That's durum wheat. It's got a beard just like barley, but the beard gets black when it ripens."

It was a hot Saskatchewan afternoon. There hadn't been enough rain for a couple of years and the crops were very poor. Don was showing me the land he'd been farming for 30 years. His voice reflected an obvious pride in that half-section of flat prairie. He talked about the short stalks on the grain and how that made the harvesting difficult, sometimes impossible.

Back at his home, we talked about the economics of farming, how the unpredictable weather, European grain subsidies, plus the inflexible banks had forced so many farmers into bankruptcy.

I had thought I knew something about farming. After all, I grew up in a farming area and spent my boyhood on my aunt and uncle's farm. But that was 50 years ago. It struck me that farming was far more complex than I imagined. The issues were not the simple ones the media had told me about. There were complexities and nuances and exceptions and variables involved in farming that were far beyond my understanding and that put the lie to my simplistic judgments.

Two days later I found myself talking to a young guide at the Head-Smashed-In heritage site near Lethbridge, Alberta. It's a huge exhibit which shows the relationship between the native people and the plains buffalo. The exhibit is built on a cliff where herds of buffalo were driven over the edge and slaughtered. A jumping pound, they called it.

I never liked the idea of driving herds of animals over a cliff. I thought of it as cruel and wasteful. And sometimes it was. But the young guide talked of her people's close and complex relationship to the buffalo and my simplistic judgments flew out the window.

I realized once again that almost everything looks much simpler when you are on the outside looking in. It's always easier to make judgments when you don't have too much information.

The same thing is true of human relationships. I know the solution to pretty well everyone's marriage difficulties except my own. As some wise person once said, "If you know the answer, you don't understand the question."

If we offer our simplistic solutions to other people's problems, they have a right to offer theirs for ours. Trading simplistic solutions does not really generate lasting friendships or anything else except a tightness near the bottom of our stomachs.

I thought about that after visiting with some friends recently. Their marriage is showing some strain. For once I kept my mouth shut and didn't offer any advice. But I did offer some love and caring. On that occasion at least, I got it right.

That's really the only thing we can offer, when other people tell us about complex problems. Quick and easy answers are the worst thing we can give. Usually it's best to not offer any answers at all. Don't judge.

Solutions are so easy. And cheap. And usually unhelpful.

Loving is hard. It's hard because we all have a tape in our heads that says, "Tell them how to fix it!"

Well, don't.

Just love one another.

A Small Silence

I think I'll become a Trappist monk and go live in a monastery where they have a rule of silence. Nobody ever talks to anyone.

I'll even throw my beloved computer in the trash can and recycle all my books and other papery paraphernalia.

They say the things you love are the things that will frustrate you, and this is certainly true of words. "Words, words, I'm so sick of words," sang Eliza Doolittle in *My Fair Lady*. My own little outburst was prompted by a frustrating discussion on the phone that turned into an argument about semantics. When I hung up the phone I found myself looking at a banner in my office that says, "Without justice there can be no peace."

"What in blazes do those words mean?" my inner cynic shouted. The person I'd been fussing with on the phone used the phrase, "It's a justice issue!" as the *coup de grace*. Claiming that makes any position the right position.

But what is a "justice issue"? People who are at polar opposites in the abortion or death penalty debates would both claim they were on the side of justice. I don't know anyone who isn't in favor of justice.

And what is "peace" for that matter? The *Pax Romana* of Jesus' day was both peaceful and just by Roman definitions. When Benito Mussolini ruled Italy with an iron fist, people said, "Well, at least we have peace and the trains run on time." When Ferdinand Marcos ruled the Philippines with his bolo-knife democracy, some Filipinos said, "For the first time, we have peace in the land." Everyone is in favor of peace, provided *they* get to define peace. Everybody wants justice, as long as *they* can decide what is just.

Words! Bah! Humbug!

What about a moratorium on words? A silly suggestion.

Here's a better one. What about a moratorium on definitions?

Better still. Suppose we stop using words as knives to slice reality into neat little pieces we can label and control, and just start acting on our own lives with what we already know.

Best suggestion of all. Let's all become Quakers. Everyone sit close together, hold hands, and let's just be with each other in silence for 15 minutes and think about those words, "justice" and "peace," and how they are lived in our lives.

Not anyone else's life. I can't do anything about you and you can't do anything about me. But we can have some effect on ourselves. So let's think about peace and justice as *we* are living it.

Silence by itself doesn't solve many problems. People who don't understand each other probably aren't going to understand each other much better after fuming quietly for 15 minutes. They might even be madder. But a focused silence, during which we look at *ourselves* and what *we* might change, is not a bad thing to try when tensions run high.

We may find a new perspective. And a little bit of quietness sometimes helps to heal a wounded soul.

No Words for This

It's springtime in the Rockies. Snow outlines the crags and peaks. A bright spring sunshine highlights every detail.

"It's beautiful! Just beautiful!" I murmur.

And it is. Of course it is. But my words say so little of sun on mountain peaks. There are no words for this.

• • •

I sit beside a friend and hold her hand while she cries for her son who has been arrested for armed robbery. When the tears have finished, I see a pain in her eyes that reflects the terror in her soul.

"Do you want to talk about it?" I ask, trying to be helpful.

A long silence. Several times she breathes as if to speak.

"There are no words for this," she says.

• • •

For the best and the worst there are no words. No words can offer more than pale approximations of glory and despair.

But sometimes in the glory and despair we catch a glimpse of God. God who knows no boundaries of names like Father, Mother, Lord, Master, Yahweh, Elohim, Creator.

All of those godly names are true, as "beautiful" is true of mountains in the springtime and "despair" is true of mothers crying for their children. But all those words are false. They squeeze the truth to fit our puny minds.

There are no words for mountains, for mothers' agony or for God.

Let's Neighbor

My Uncle Henry could toss sunflower seeds into one side of his mouth, spit the seeds out the other side, and talk at the same time. He'd never miss a syllable or a seed.

As a small town boy growing up in a tiny Russian Mennonite community, I considered Uncle Henry's skill the supreme achievement, and I resolved I'd be able to do the same thing when I grew up.

I can't. I can't even hull sunflower seeds in my mouth when I put them in carefully, one at a time. And talking is out of the question.

But I learned something more important than how to eat sunflower seeds. I learned the value of all those conversations, stories, yarns, trivia, which Uncle Henry and all the extended family and friends shared with each other in those days before TV. Talk was the major entertainment. But it was more.

When those Mennonite folks sat around to chat, they used a word for it that was very different from what we use in English. They never called it gossiping. They didn't use words like "natter" or "prattle" or "small talk" or "hanging out" or even "chatting."

The word was *nobah* which literally translates, "neighbor." *Nobah* could be either a noun or a verb. When you sit and talk to each other, just for the sake of talking to each other, you are "neighboring." It's the activity that turns an acquaintance into a neighbor. It's the recognition that small things – the leak in the roof, the child just learning to walk, the state of the garden – the sharing of these small coins of human currency build community.

"Take care of the pennies and the pounds will take care of themselves," is an old British saying. Translate that into human relationships and it means that the little things of life are sometimes more important than the big things. The "insignificant" things we say to our family over breakfast are far more important than the big gifts we may give on a birthday. The casual conversation over coffee may be more important than the big speech we make. The visit over the back fence may be more important than the community meeting.

Which is not to say that we shouldn't give due attention to the larger issues. If you're invited to address the Rotary Club, you prepare. It is possible to be "penny wise and pound foolish." But it is also true that paying attention to the tiny relationships, the small conversations, is the glue that holds the community together. The only way to build or keep a relationship is to spend time together talking about stupid small stuff.

So! Suggestion number 437 to make the world a better place for children, old people, and dogs. Let's learn from the Mennonites and use "neighbor" as both a noun and a verb. When we gather at the coffee shop or in the office lunch room – when we stand on the street corner and chat, let's make sure we're "neighboring."

Not just flapping our gums, but building community. Tell stories. Make sure you care about the person you are talking with.

And add a bag of sunflower seeds. It'll help you neighbor.

Concrete and Caterpillars

Here's two little items just oozing upright, moral messages. See if you get the connection.

• • •

I watched them pour the driveway to our house. The workers laid down steel rods, then as they poured the cement, they pulled the rods up so they would be in the middle of the concrete as it hardened.

"What do you need the rods for?" I asked one of the workers.

"It makes the concrete stronger. Reinforced concrete."

"Yes, I know, but *how* do the rods make the concrete stronger?"

The worker picked up one of the rods. "Look, if you push down on it, it bends real easy." His muscles bulged and the rod bent. "But you couldn't pull it apart. This hunk of rod could pull that truck over there. On the other hand, a piece of concrete is easy to pull apart. But if you push down on it, it won't bend."

"So?"

"So they've got opposite strengths. The steel is strong when you pull, the concrete is strong when you push. Put them together, and you've got reinforced concrete which is strong both ways. That's how they make all those big buildings and bridges. Concrete by itself or steel by itself wouldn't be strong enough."

• • •

John Henry Fabre was a French naturalist who did an experiment with some Processionary Caterpillars. Those poor little beasties will follow the next caterpillar ahead of them, no matter where that caterpillar happens to be going.

Fabre arranged a bunch of his fuzzy friends in a neat circle, each one touching the one just ahead. Faithful to their DNA, each one followed the next one. In the middle of the circle Fabre put some of the caterpillars' favorite food. Would they stop following, even for a moment, just for a bite of lunch? Not on your life.

The food was there within inches, but they just kept on following each other in circles until they collapsed and died from hunger.

• • •

The moral of those two little stories, boys and girls, is that you shouldn't hang around too much with people you agree with or with people who are too much like you.

Take me, as a really good bad example. I love hanging out with people like me who are strong on creativity and short on self-discipline. We know all the old songs and remember all the bad jokes and we can have a wonderful time belly-aching about all the same politicians. We whine about all the same institutions.

It's great fun, but we're like Dr. Fabre's caterpillars going around in circles, following each other's hind ends. It's really comfortable, but intellectually, we starve to death.

It's fun being with like-minded, creative people, and nothing upsets us as much as someone who insists on being practical – who starts writing down numbers and working out flow charts.

Of course, if you have a bunch of number crunchers and flow-chart people sitting around by themselves, you will wind up with lots of numbers and charts, but nothing much else. Dr. Fabre's caterpillars again.

However, if you can put the two kinds of folk together, and help them understand how much they need each other, things can really happen. The trouble is, their first instinct is to scratch each other's eyes out. It's really hard to get two people with opposite characteristics to genuinely appreciate each other and work together. Especially if they're married to each other.

Bev and I know that. Let me tell you, we know that!

Our personalities are polar opposite, and one of the wonders of the world is that we are still married after almost 40 years.

I could give you dozens of examples, but two will do.

Bev is the planner in our family. She does her Christmas shopping in October, if not before. I am the dreamer. I do my Christmas shopping on December 24th. If then.

When we're traveling through an unfamiliar city, it's really important that I drive and Bev navigates. She works best plotting the route and telling me, "It'd be good if you got into the left lane because the motel where I booked a room three months ago is on the left just up ahead." I seem to do better with the emerging situations of city traffic and can make the quick decisions without becoming apoplectic.

However, if we reverse the roles – if Bev drives and I plan the trip and navigate – within half an hour we are parked in a no-parking zone having what the police call "a domestic altercation."

When we are ready to acknowledge our own weaknesses and appreciate other people's complementary strength – when we are ready to listen to ideas and opinions we've never thought of before – then we can stop going around in tight little circles and build the temple we dreamed of.

Or at least find the motel before midnight.

In Defense of Slavery

Growing up in southern Manitoba, we always kept a cow for milk. Each spring when the cow went out to pasture, Dad and I would check the electric fence and connect the battery. One or two shocks on her snout as she grazed and Bossy would give the fence a wide birth. We'd disconnect the battery but the cow would never go near the fence again.

One year a car, careening off the road, took out our fence. We didn't get around to fixing it all summer. And all summer, Bossy looked longingly at the alfalfa field across the road, but she never crossed the line where the fence had been.

I'm not much impressed with the intelligence of cows.

I'm not much impressed with human intelligence either.

Years ago, when they first invented the typewriter, they discovered the keys would stick if you hit them too quickly, one after the other. So they arranged the keys in such a way that it would slow down the typists.

Now, I'm typing this on a modern computer with a keyboard that can take the signals 50 times faster than I can type them, but I'm still using the keyboard layout invented years ago to slow folks down.

The standard typewriter or computer keyboard was arranged to solve a problem that doesn't exist anymore. And I'm a slave to that system, even though I know there are layouts invented that could increase my typing speed dramatically. I could convert my keyboard to the new system. I could take the time to learn it. But I'm much too lazy to change.

Our ecological, social and political problems are not caused by a lack of knowledge. We know what to do.

But oh, it's so much easier just to slither along in the rut we know. Slavery is so much more comfortable than freedom.

182 • Angels in Red Suspenders

You're Second Rate, So Accept That

The journey to enlightenment is long. So very long.

I was deeply grateful to my guru who had been so patient as I struggled to ready my mind, my body, my soul to hear the answer to my agonized cry, "What, oh what is the problem with our country?" Several times she told me how patient she was being.

My heart pounded in my chest. An acrid stench assaulted my nose. "Damn," I said. "Deodorant breakdown again. That's twice this week."

My guru smiled a slight smile which, on a lesser mortal, might have been interpreted as a smirk, as she walked slowly into the Chamber of Wisdom where we had been meeting each day for a month. "Sit down, child," she said firmly. "Are you quite prepared to hear the answer to your question?"

"I am, oh divine one."

She gazed for an eternity into the candle before her. Finally she spoke. I leaned forward to catch every precious word.

"Here is the illness of our country," she said. "In our country, they put leaders into positions of leadership."

"Yes?" I said, expecting more.

"That's it. They put leaders into positions of leadership. That's the problem with our country."

"But," I sputtered, "where else would you put leaders. Into followership?"

"Yes," she smiled. Or smirked. "Now you have achieved enlightenment."

"Then who should lead?"

"The followers."

"But how can followers lead?"

"Because they understand what following means. Leaders don't know anything about that. But in the world of wisdom that is to come, the first shall be last and the last shall be first. Whoever would be first among you must be like the least of these. That's all original you know."

"But Miss Guru ma'am...."

"Ms. Guru please."

"Ms. Guru, leaders are smarter than followers. Don't leaders know better than followers?"

"Of course they know better. That's why leaders are not equipped to lead. They don't know what it means to be a plodder."

"Plodder?"

"Correct, you dolt. Most people in our country are plodders. That includes most government workers. They play with a full deck but they don't have any trumps or aces. The leaders, the cabinet, have all those, and they use them. And the plodders keep wondering if they're playing the same ball game."

"You're mixing your metaphors."

"Shut up. I'm the guru. You're the guree. And you're a plodder. Don't try to be brilliant. Or creative, or even to work very hard. You're second rate, so just accept that."

"Oh thank you, great Guru, for that hard teaching."

"Don't mention it. In our country, the leaders dream up ideas and write things and make speeches and do reports and all that neatsy stuff. The leaders develop the resources which the followers don't understand. They do analysis that leaves the plodders cold. The leaders make "collegial" decisions without inviting the followers into the college. In short, the leaders are playing with all the aces. Then they throw their hand on the table and the follower is caught with nothing but a pair of nines."

"So what do we do?"

"Do like Chairman Mao. Send all your eggheads and all your mandarins out to stand ankle deep in the cow barn, and have them do a bit of shoveling."

"And the followers would lead?"

"No, but they'd go through the motions."

"And our country would stand still. It wouldn't make any progress."

"True, but you asked about the problem and that's it. No leaders, no problems. Everybody would understand everyone. Perfect communication. No leaders out there miles ahead and out of sight."

"Our country would die."

"To die is to have no more problems."

"Is there another way?"

"Yes."

"What is it?"

"That is wisdom only for the leaders. You are not a leader. That wisdom is too much for you and besides you can't afford it. Just be a slob and be content."

"Oh thank you great guru, for that even harder teaching."

Admired Everywhere, Except at Home

You need to know about King Ludwig, because he's a really good bad example.

Ludwig was the Hugh Heffner of his day, the playboy champion of the "if it feels good, do it" philosophy. He ruled in Bavaria until he died in 1886. He left behind a string of castles, one of which became the model for Walt Disney's famous fairy-tale castle.

Ludwig's castles defy description. They are big. They are certainly not beautiful, but they are certainly decorated. Decorated and over-decorated. In every nook and cranny, on every inch of floor, wall and corner of ceiling, there is carving and painting and decoration of the most intricate and clever variety. There's gold leaf, delicate crystal and ceramics, fine oil painting, inlaid wood and ivory. On the ceiling above Ludwig's bed, there's an extremely well done fresco, featuring a variety of nubile nudes in what can only be described as soft-core porn. It takes a long time to get tourists to move from the bedroom to the dining room.

The dining room has even more decoration, if that's possible. But the most interesting feature is the disappearing table.

Ludwig didn't like people much. Especially anyone still alive. Especially servants. So he had the servants set his feast on the table down in the basement, and then crank it up through the floor.

Often Ludwig had the table set for two, even though he was by himself. The servants could hear him in conversation with famous beautiful women with whom he was in love. That would have been very nice, except all of the women he loved were dead.

Ludwig was famous throughout the world. He was admired everywhere. Everywhere, except in Bavaria, because he paid for his extravagant castles by sucking the country dry.

King Ludwig, along with his personal physician, drowned in three feet of water. Ludwig was seven feet tall.

A Patron Saint

I would like to nominate the Reverend Dr. William Archibald Spooner (1844-1930) as the patron saint of after dinner speakers. Also preachers. And those poor sad souls trying to be articulate at Toastmaster's meetings. There's probably already such a patron saint, but Spooner, I think, is more eminently qualified than any other person could possibly be.

Consider. Spooner did a reasonably creditable job. He worked hard, paid his dues, did all the things he should have done. Julian Huxley (brother of Aldous) described him as a "good scholar and a good teacher," who had "that rare quality which I can only describe as saintliness." And yet Spooner is most remembered for a few occasions when he tripped over his words, got his "tang all tonguled." He gave a name to the transpositional gaffes that offer delight to hearers but despair to the utterers. Spoonerisms.

Show me a speaker who has given more than a talk or two, and I'll show you a person who has had at least a mild case of Spooner's "moot-in-fouth disease." Spooner was not the first nor the last to suffer from that affliction, nor was his case much worse than that infecting many speakers. But once the stories began, the legend took off. And it soon outstripped reality.

Spooner really admitted to only one spoonerism. Announcing the hymn "Conquering Kings their Titles Take," he apparently said, "Kinkering Congs..."

The legend might have been contained, except that Spooner taught at New College, Oxford, and the Reverend doctor's occasional "clerical errors" got the stories going, and soon campus comedians began inventing "spoonerisms."

Here are a few of the gaffes attributed to the poor, unfortunate Spooner.

"Blushing crow" for "crushing blow." At a wedding he is presumed to have said, "it is kisstomary to cuss the bride." In his sermons Spooner is said to have referred to "tearful chidings" when he meant "cheerful tidings," and "From Greenlands Icy Mountains," was transformed to "From Iceland's greasy mountains." The prodigal son was "on the 'busy drink' of destruction," and he assured his congregation that "the Lord is a 'shoving leopard' (loving shepherd)."

One Sunday evening Spooner is said to have sighed, "It is beery work preaching to empty wenches."

Spooner could have used a more developed sense of humor to protect himself from the students at Oxford. If he'd had the grace to be amused at the real gaffes as well as at the legend, life would have been much easier for him. As it was, he railed and fumed at the stories developing around him, which of course fed the fiction. Spooner lacked the grace to laugh at himself, and it cost him dearly.

He left a great gift he didn't intend and mostly hated. By giving his name to this common linguistic malady, Spooner helped us become aware that we all suffer from it occasionally or often, and that the only antidote is laughter. When spoonerisms were named, the language experts began describing and cataloguing them, so that folks like me could occasionally use them to good effect and add a bit of spice to an otherwise dull and unconvincing narrative.

Of course, the best spoonerisms come as a surprise to the speaker. Reading a commercial on the radio for some long-forgotten medication, I asked, "Do you sometimes feel dill and lustless?" And on another occasion I transposed "rug and drape shop" to, you guessed it, "drug and rape shop." And in an inspiring speech at a graduation, I invited the students at one point to "wound our heels" and a little later to "fail into the suture." It was not one of my best speeches.

So let us name the good Dr. Spooner the "satron paint" of public speakers and celebrate his birthday, July 22nd, with a "21 sun galute."

Let's mark the day with "spoons full of speacherisms," beginning perhaps with the grand-daddy of them all committed by an announcer for the Canadian Broadcasting Corporation following the broadcast of a church service. "Next week, the sermon will be titled, 'Cast thy broad upon the waters.' This is the Canadian Bread Corping Castration."

The Printer's Devil

I never make misteaks.

Sure, I sometimes invent a few creative variations that drive editors and proofreaders wild. But errors? Never!

Mistakes, like beauty, are in the eye of the beholder. I never notice any mistakes so I don't make any.

This tradition of literary creativity has a long history. In 1561, a racy little volume of 172 pages called *Missae ac Missalis Anatomia* was printed with 15 pages of *errata*.

The pious monk who wrote this little book explained that the devil hated his work so much, that in the middle of the night, Old Nick had relieved himself on the manuscript, making the ink run and therefore difficult to read. Which gave rise to the tradition of the "printer's devil." This tradition holds that no matter how hard you try, the first thing you will notice when the book comes off the press is a glaring error. This is especially true if you are either the publisher or the author.

"Not so!" proclaimed Foulis, the famed 18th-century Glasgow publishers. "We will produce the perrrfect book. Without errrorrr." Only the Scots would dream of producing a book which would be a perfect specimen of typographical accuracy.

That a book should first of all be interesting and worth reading is not an argument they considered relevant.

Six experienced proofreaders were employed who went over every dot and tittle (Does anyone know what tittles are?) of this absolutely error-free book Foulis set out to publish. Then they posted the galleys in the hallowed halls of Glasgow U. with a reward of £50 to anyone who could find an error.

When they finally released this perfect book they found an error on the first line of the first page.

Murphy may be Irish, but he lives in Glasgow. And in Winfield, B.C.

Years ago when the tiny, neophyte publishing house called Wood Lake Books produced its very first book, *The Gift of Story* by yours truly, I set the type myself and then commandeered a group of women from St. Paul's United Church to proofread the book. The theory was that even though none of them were professional proofreaders, if enough of them went through the blessed thing, they should find all the mistakes.

It's not a theory that works out in practice. For one thing, whenever you correct a mistake, you have a very good chance of making another. This was in the olden days before computers, when you had to retype the whole line, sometimes the whole paragraph, to correct one spelling error.

When we had flailed away at the book till we were all sick and tired of it, I decided to declare it corrected. But that night I thought it would be only proper to thank the women who had worked so hard to find my many mistakes.

So I typed a paragraph in the foreword thanking the "profreaders."

Be a Brain Surgeon in Your Spare Time

Two guys are sitting next to each other on an airplane. Being males, they soon get to the status question. What are you? In other words, what is the pecking order here?

"I'm a brain surgeon," said the one.

"I'm a writer," said the other.

"That's interesting," said the first. "I've been thinking of becoming a writer when I retire."

"Fascinating," said the writer. "I've been thinking of becoming a brain surgeon when I retire."

Did you find that amusing? Even slightly? Was it amusing when the brain surgeon said he wanted to be a writer when he retired, or was it the part about the writer being a brain surgeon? Brain surgeons can be writers, but not the other way around. Right?

That assumption makes me and other word-smiths very twitchy. We may have spent as many years and worked as hard at stroking the significance out of words and ideas and concepts as that brain surgeon did learning how to cut open people's craniums. But the surgeon thinks he can learn writing from a how-to book he buys at Waldons. Does Waldons carry a do-it-yourself lobotomy book? Yet the talent of a Shakespeare writing "Out! Out, brief candle..." is as awesome as that of anyone who ever probed a *corpus callosum*.

I am writing this on the deck of a cruise ship, well into the second day of eating my way up the Inside Passage of Canada's spectacular west coast. The computer programmer in the deck chair next to me has gone to get some lunch and left me here with my laptop and torn between my fascination with words and my fascination with the magnificence I see.

I'm not getting a whole lot of work done.

The computer programmer was a nice guy and we had a good conversation. He told me about a lawyer relative who wrote a book, then got his shirt in a knot because he couldn't find a publisher. "You'd think a lawyer could find a publisher," said my new friend. That's when the story about the brain surgeon came out. I told him that most lawyers I know use human language about as well as Sumo wrestlers do needlepoint.

Writers are insecure and neurotic (as well as underpaid and under recognized) and feel that as a species, we are persecuted and maligned. That's because writing a really good essay or poem is like peeing your pants while wearing a dark suit. It gives you a warm feeling but nobody notices. A writer's task is to notice truth and put words around it. Not to define truth but to point to it so that others too may notice. Nothing more.

But, God help us, nothing less!

Writers use words, a resource of which there is unlimited supply. We use the same words everyone uses, but when we get it right, the emotions, the feelings, the concepts, the images, the ideas are distilled with clarity and force. Then nobody notices our words. We fuss for hours trying to find exactly the cadence, the right subtleties of tone and nuance to hold the power, the pain, the wonder that is life. It's transparent. If we succeed and people see that wonder, nobody notices us. When someone says, "Gee, that's great writing," it hardly ever is. Like cleaning a window. When you do it right, the light shines through and you don't notice the glass.

Words are mysterious and hidden in their working, but words surround us continually. We hear them pouring out of our own mouths and from the folk around us. Words assault our eyes from billboards and our ears from TV sets and PA systems. "Talk is

192 • Angels in Red Suspenders

cheap," and so is writing. One of the questionable benefits of computers is that we can churn out quantities of words so much more easily. But quality words that are savored and treasured are just as precious and rare as ever. Perhaps more so. And harder to find in that weedpatch of computer verbiage.

Words that distill truth cut through our consciousness and affect us far more deeply than any brain surgeon's incision. "The pen is mightier than the sword," and sharper than the scalpel. When a dictator takes over a country, it's the writers who are jailed first, not the doctors. It's the media that describe our social reality, not the lawyers or physicians.

Writers, like artists and preachers of all kinds, work with ideas and concepts – with truth and falsehood – with the stuff that defines a person or a nation. The writer's playthings are the viruses of a social disease that drains a people of their spiritual energy or purges its bureaucratic bowels of deceit. And the best writers have a built-in bullshit detector, which makes it almost impossible for them to write for the popular media.

Whatever else it is, good writing is not a pastime to be picked up at will and played with. The urge to write is a curse perhaps. A yoke. A burden. A disease. A passion.

But writing is never a hobby.

The Gender Wars

Real Liberation

I read Bev a story out of the newspaper about the two guys in Texas who made a medieval catapult big enough to toss a Buick 200 yards.

"Boy, I'd love to see that!" I said.

"Why in the world would they want to do that?" she asked.

Bev and I gave each other one of those, "Are you nuts or something?" looks.

The incident is only important because it points to a continuing problem. Women and men regard each other as "perceptually challenged."

Bev thinks it's important that our bed should be made. In the morning. Before breakfast. Every day. Even if we're not expecting company.

She gives me that "typical man" look whenever I point out that we're going to mess it up again that very evening, and if somebody should pop over unexpectedly, we can shut the bedroom door.

This is not a point of discussion or negotiation. This is the two sexes seeing reality from opposite sides of different worlds. "Explaining to a man why the bed should be made is like explaining to a bullfrog why you enjoy Mozart," a feminist friend once said. I don't think she understood it from the male point of view which is...well...just the male point of view, that's all.

I heard on the radio once that you can tell whether a married couple is liberated by who makes the bed. The person didn't say whether I was liberated if Bev made the bed or she would be liberated if I made the bed, or what. Being a member of the most logical sex (We are so!) I would assert that the person most capable of making the bed, should do it. Right? It makes sense. Well, it makes sense to any male, that's for sure.

Bev, after all, was trained as a young girl to make beds. With a flip and a tug and a pat she can have the damn thing done in no time flat.

Please understand, I am a totally liberated male. I'm not against males occasionally making beds. I did it myself, once. I don't think it substantially jeopardized my masculinity. But, as a male, I'm not suited to the job. Whenever I flip one of the sheets, it flops in the wrong direction. If I tug, it pulls out from wherever I've tucked in. My pats are mostly a desperate last-ditch attempt to flatten the lumps underneath.

So it would seem reasonable that Bev should always make the bed.

Bev, however, seems to feel that since I messed up at least 50 percent of it, I should straighten out at least 50 percent of it. And, yes, there is a kind of logic about that. It's not in the same league as my logic, you understand, but she does have a point.

And I am a noble, understanding, considerate (and modest) man. "Okay honey, you make your side, and I'll make mine." It's a great theory. It doesn't work.

At least not if she makes her side at a different time than I'm making my side, because whoever does it last unmakes the side that was made first.

It does work, however, if you do it at the same time, and develop a bit of intricate teamwork so that you both tug the sheets just the right amount to pull them tight without yanking them out of your partner's hand. Flip, tug, pat! In about half of two shakes you can have it done. Actually kind of fun and satisfying.

Maybe real liberation, and genuine logic, is doing it together.

In the Boardroom and the Bedroom

Surprise! Women and men are different. And spare me the bath-room humor – I'm not talking about plumbing here.

Guys, I don't know how to break this to you. What the sci-entific folks have been finding out about gender differences is good news in the short run, but by the year 2020, women will have a decided edge. That's because all the things men do best and most easily can now be done by machines. Mostly comput-ers. What women do best and most easily will still be done by humans. So guess who's going to be in charge of the world?

This is very dangerous territory, and people like me who talk publicly on such matters tend to have a short life expectancy. So the first thing that needs to be said very loudly is that there's a huge spectrum of characteristics within both males and females. What I'm talking about is averages, which is *really* dangerous, because nobody is really ever "average." Or "normal."

In a room full of people, the tallest one may well be a woman, but on average, men are taller. If you put Margaret Thatcher and Jean Vanier on a male/female characteristics continuum, Vanier would be well on the female side and Thatcher well on the male. So don't quote me as saying, "All males are this..." or "all females are that." We're talking averages here, which means we have to be very careful not to put people in pigeon holes.

So. Men. Listen up. We generally – not always but generally – do better at things involving muscle bulk, hand-eye coordination, and rational, logical, left-brained calculations. That's why so many of us are into hockey, weight lifting and computers. That's also why so many of us are infantile when it comes to human relationships. That's why so many of us act like scared little boys who go around trying to talk like Don Cherry, the world's most obsolete male.

Women. You most often – not always, but most often – do better at understanding and, if you choose to, manipulating human relationships. Also at communicating ideas and concepts (as opposed to raw facts). In both the boardroom and the bedroom, you are far more likely to know what is really going on. Guess who has the upper hand in the new millennium?

Yes, I know I said all the things men used to do with muscle bulk will be done by machines run by computers, and yes, men love to play with computers and are good at it. But more and more, Bill Gates and his cronies are using computers to develop better computers, and computers to program computers, and all those hackers won't have anything to do except exchange trivia on the Internet. Meanwhile the percentage of women on the Internet and involved in computers generally, is increasing daily, and it is less and less a boy's preserve.

All of this is proving scientifically what we've hunched all along. When Bev and I go out for an evening with friends, she picks up all kinds of subtle information that I don't even notice. When it comes to understanding other people, I am, as the PCPs (politically correct people) say, perceptually challenged.

Most men don't know this, but women exchange "dumb male" jokes the way the guys used to exchange "dumb blond" jokes a few years ago. "What do you call a man with half a brain? Gifted!"

We could shrug those off, but the jokes are funny because there is a germ of truth in every one of them. Bev is right. I was born blind. I simply don't see the hurt in people's eyes. I simply don't see the anger under the calm exterior.

That's scary. If men are less likely to see the human issues – the relationship issues and hence the justice issues, why do we keep choosing males to run our governments? If it's true that men have a tendency to be blind to justice issues, then Clinton and Chretien and Major and Yeltsin may be, like me, perceptually challenged. Show them an oppressed person, and they see an economic or political problem. They don't see a hurting human. It's no good yelling at them. They were born blind.

Which does not mean we men cannot be given sight. It takes a miracle, but miracles do happen. There are thousands of men who have learned to see. That's the good news. We men are not so handicapped that we can't learn, if we want to. Or if we can't learn, then at least we might trust the judgment of someone who *can* see.

John Newton was born blind (though his eyes worked fine). Newton was a successful slave trader, who saw the African people only as a commodity to be traded and used. Then amazing grace burst into his life, and he was given the gift of sight. One day, Newton looked into the eyes of one of his slave cargo and saw a human being – a child of God.

Years later, he wrote the hymn which became a pop-chart hit:

I once was lost, but now am found.
Was blind, but now I see.

Take heart, guys. We don't need to become obsolete. My spies tell me that, generally speaking, the women want to keep us around.

It's going to be tough. It's a steep learning curve.

But we can do it. We can learn to see.

Wrestling with God

Wrestling is very much a male metaphor. It's a metaphor for the way we encounter other men. It's a metaphor for the way we encounter God. Most women don't like it.

A friend, who wrestles weekly at the "Y" says it is one of the few socially acceptable ways men can touch other male bodies in intimacy. "And we always hope," he said, "that we can learn to love each other before we kill each other."

I don't understand that anymore. I don't know if I ever did, since wrestling, or any other competitive sport, was never part of my reality. I was no good at sports, so I avoided them and competed intellectually, instead.

And I miss it. There is a deep "skin-hunger" a profound, though usually suppressed desire to be touched by people of both genders, and it is only marginally related to sexuality. Or at least to coitus.

We lived in the Philippines for a number of years, where men routinely and openly express their affection for each other by hugging and holding hands and even kissing. For a Canadian kid raised on the idea that men express their affection by punching each other on the shoulder, I found that really hard.

I will never forget the day Ernesto Songco and I were walking down the street and he took my hand. Ernesto and I had become friends and for him it was a natural, easy thing to do. My backbone froze. I found myself glancing around to see if anybody was looking and it was all I could do to keep from pulling my hand away in horror. But over the years we lived in the Philippines, I grew to appreciate that expression of friendship from men and to enjoy it. I began to find it easy to take the hand of a male friend as we walked together. Now that we're back in North America, I miss it. All my homophobic reflexes kicked in as soon as the plane hit the tarmac.

My friend is right though. In our western European tradition, for men to be close they must fight. Like kittens and puppies, it is how we learn. It's how we develop. It may be mock conflict – ritualized conflict – but there needs to be stress and tension and body straining against body. Or mind against mind. Tension creates strength and struggle develops skill, and that may be most true in the arena of spiritual growth.

There is a very ancient legend of Jacob, the Hebrew patriarch, who spent most of his younger life cheating people and running away from the consequences. He diddled his brother Esau out of the family inheritance, then ran. But years later, with the load of guilt on his shoulders, he finally decided he needed to be reconciled with his brother before he could get on with his life.

Just before he was to meet his brother, Jacob spent the night beside the river Jabbok, and there he dreamed that he was wrestling with a man, and the man turned out to be God, and they wrestled all night without either one winning. Just before dawn, the God-man told Jacob, "Your name will no longer be Jacob (the cheater) but will be Israel, the one who wrestles with God." Then the God-man threw Jacob's hip out of joint, and Jacob woke up screaming. But the dream was real, and Jacob walked limping toward his brother and the future.

So often we think of meeting God in a quiet little chat by a mountain stream or in a country chapel. But as often as not, God tackles us, throws us to the ground, wounds us, and then gives us a new name, a new direction, and sends us limping toward our future.

If I live long enough, like another 50 years maybe, I will fulfill a lifetime ambition to go across the country, sit down with clergy and collect stories. Most of the stories will be about weddings and funerals. I hang around with clergy enough to know there are a million stories, and most of them are good.

The wedding stories will be funny, winsome, hilarious.

But the funeral stories will often be poignant. The funeral stories will often be Jacob-at-the-Jabbok stories; of God and humanity in combat; of humans screaming in pain when God touches their tender places; of people turning their lives around and God giving them a new name; a purpose.

I would want to hear stories such as the one about Jason, the lawyer whose daughter died from anorexia nervosa, a terrifying psychological disease. His daughter literally starved herself to death, and the guilt and anger this man felt brought him close to suicide. But there were other children in the family, and a spouse who was both caring and competent, and they rallied around him. He quit the high-pressure law firm that kept him working all hours and now runs a food bank for less than one-quarter his previous salary. Together they are rebuilding their family from the ground up.

This man is one of the wounded people. Like women and men down through the centuries, he has wrestled with God. Now he has a new identity – and he walks with a limp. But he has the power to break the loaves and distribute the fishes and teach compassion to the world.

Wrestling isn't the only metaphor for our encounter with God. But it's a good one.

Something to Brag About

I turn off the TV in disgust when the hockey game degenerates into a street brawl. If that's what I wanted, I'd have turned on exhibition wrestling. Feeling cynical and disappointed, I turn my computer on and write words I only sometimes believe.

• • •

The basic function of war and sports is to give the guys something to brag about in the bars; something they can understand. Some women will tell you that males are congenitally unable to understand anything more subtle than a hockey stick in the groin or a club on the head, and sometimes I think they may be right. If the women are right, war and sports are essential to human survival. Well, male survival, anyway. The issues are clear and understandable.

Every fall, we get geared up for Grey Cup day, the Canadian equivalent to the Super Bowl. Every fall, I find myself wondering if this national bacchanalia is simply ritualized warfare. Every fall, my friends who are in counseling work tell me there will be more spousal abuse following major national contact sports championships than at any time except Christmas and New Year's.

Does anything ever really change?

Mostly I am an optimistic and hopeful person, but the other day I found myself talking to one of those spouses who looks forward to the Grey Cup the way I look forward to a root canal.

She got me feeling pretty cynical, and I found myself saying, "No. We've changed the name and fixed the rules a little, but the lust for violence we bring to contact sports is not much different than the lust for violence that motivated our warring forefathers."

As documentary evidence, I refer you to the books called First and Second Samuel in the Bible, the books that tell the stories of Kings Saul and David. They read like the sports pages in your newspapers – who beat whom and how badly.

To demonstrate, I've done a very slight re-write of the story of David and Goliath – a story that's in the Bible, because for years, when the guys in Jerusalem got together for a couple of drinks, that's what they talked about.

"Hey, Esau. How about them Israelites, eh?"

"Hoooeee! Jeez, you shoulda seen little Davey take that big guy's head off." And other uplifting stuff.

The "message" of this biblical story is simply that "our guys are tougher than your guys," but it keeps getting told in churches and Sunday schools as if it had some deep religious significance.

Well, it's in the Bible so it must have a profound spiritual meaning, right?

Wrong!

• • •

"Hey Davey. Do your old dad a favor, will ya."

"What now?" David was never very enthusiastic when his dad asked him to do something. Two weeks ago he'd asked David to look after the sheep. "Asked," was the wrong word. "Told," was more like it.

David hated sheep. Dumbest animals in the world. Good for only two things. They got clipped and they got eaten. But David kept planning on the day he could get out of Bethlehem and play in the big leagues – the Mediterranean wars. All he needed was just one chance to show how good he was. In the meantime, he did push-ups and sit-ups and worked on his hand-eye coordination.

"Davey," said his Dad. "I got your mom to pack a lunch for your brothers. I want you to take it to them. Go find out what the score is in the fight against the Philistines and come back and tell me."

"All right!" yelled David. He'd been itching to get to see some action against the Philistines. So he was underage. So what? Maybe this was his chance.

David ran into the house, grabbed the sack held out by his mother and ran off toward the valley where they were having the war.

When David got there, and it was a fair hike, nothing was happening. No fighting, no nothing. All the guys were sitting around looking like they'd just swallowed rotten eggs.

"Hey, what's happening?" David asked. "What's the score?"

"Score? It's Philistines zip, Israelites zip. It's all tied up and we've had two sudden death overtime periods, now we're into the one-on-one shoot-out."

"So what's the problem?"

"Problem? Take a look at that Philistine over there. The big guy wearing number 99. His name's Goliath. Would you go one-on-one with him?"

"Jeez," said David. "What a jock! But I bet I could beat him."

"You? You're half his size. Gimme a break! Besides the coach wouldn't let you. Did they call you up from the farm team?"

David was a cocky little character. Off he went to talk to the coach Saul. "Coach, look, I know I'm small, and I'm from the bush league, but I've got some moves that big old 99 out there doesn't know. He's huge, but all those steroids make him a bit soft in the head. I'm small, but I'm smart and I'm fast."

Well, coach Saul didn't have a lot of options. All the guys on the front of his bench were freaked out by this Goliath. "Here," said Saul. "Put on my pads and my helmet."

David tried them on, but took them off again. "Too big and too heavy, Saul," said David. "I gotta be free to be me."

"This is insane," said coach Saul, "but the kid's the only one crazy enough to go one-on-one with that gorilla."

Goliath almost split a gut laughing when he saw the kid coming up against him, swinging his puny little slingshot. But little Davey deaked Goliath right out of his socks, put a move on him he'd never seen before, and scored the game winning point.

Israelites 1. Philistines 0. Final score.

Davey became an instant superstar. Everybody's hero. Saul offered him a fat contract and lined him up for a heavy date with his daughter. Saul's beefy son Jonathan got the hots for David too, and started giving him expensive presents. Advertisers pushed and shoved to sign David up for lucrative endorsements.

David's Dad sent a message. "Hey, come home Davey. You've got to look after your sheep."

What Davey said to his dad is best not recorded.

• • •

Make up your own mind. Blow the dust off that old family Bible and check 1 Samuel 17. Is there any fundamental difference between those wars and the Super Bowl?

Sorry to be so cynical. It's the time of year.

The Squeak in My Psyche

The folks at the table next to us had been on the helicopter. Those sharing our table had been on the float plane trip. All of them had gone swooping and soaring through the mists of Juneau, Alaska, delighting in the crystal blue of the Mendenhall Glacier.

Bev and I went on the bus. We also saw the mists of Juneau and the Mendenhall Glacier, but we kept in touch with good old *terra ferma*. I have acquired in my dotage a good case of acrophobia – the fear of heights. All the huskies in Alaska could not have put me on a small aircraft or a helicopter to view all seven wonders of the world. Especially, they would not get me on the cable car they are building in Juneau.

So as our table mates on the cruise ship wax ecstatic about their adventures Bev and I sit in silence, and I wonder if Bev would have done the plane trip if she didn't have me hanging onto her skirts. She'll never tell me.

It's a disease of age. Or at least it gets worse as you "mature." I never much liked heights, even as a child. Oh, I could climb ladders and trees with my friends, but secretly I hated it. It didn't seem as bad then. I did a lot of things then I wouldn't do now, not all of them involving heights.

Each Halloween, my friends and I would dream up one really neat "trick of the year." Once about a dozen of us moved the big municipal road grader onto old man Schröder's front yard. Another year, we decided that tipping outhouses was too boring, so we moved them back four feet, just behind the hole. There was hell to pay for that one.

The year it was decided to dismantle a buggy and reassemble it on the roof of the local grain elevator, I opted out. I made some lame excuses, but all my buds knew I was simply too "chicken." (They did it too. They got the buggy up there and put it back together, and for years I told the story as if I was part of it.)

It is possible to cure acrophobia. My good friend Frank, a psychiatrist, tells me there are therapies I could do, but I've been in denial too long to change now. I tell all the world I am a 100 percent totally well-balanced, well-adjusted, self-aware and utterly healthy male who doesn't need help from nobody. See! That's my story, and I plan to stick to it.

Well, except for one or two minor things. Like acrophobia.

I've managed to sublimate the phobia when it comes to flying planes. The bigger the better. From our small city in the Okanagan Valley, the airlines fly little eggbeaters which have almost enough leg room for a vertically challenged midget – propeller jobs that vibrate and roar like badly tuned Sherman tanks. The fetal position I'm forced into by the tiny seats feels quite appropriate, actually, because when we take off, the voice in the back of my head is yelling, "These things can't fly! You are going to crash! For sure this time!" Then we hit a minor air pocket and the voice yells, "See!"

I fly a lot in the course of my work. Bev and I travel recreationally. I've put a plug in the face of that scared kid inside me. That is, until something happens. Like when the sound of the engine changes just before we come down to land. The kid screams inside me, "This is it. Say your prayers." But I am a man, right? If you were sitting beside me on the plane, you'd think I was Joe Cool. All that agony is going on quietly about eight inches below my rib cage.

I pay no attention to that frightened pip-squeak. I shove him down inside my psyche and nobody ever knows. Nobody.

Except for times when that squeamish kid pops out to surprise me. On my study trip to Israel, we visited the famous ruins of Masada, which are way up on top of a mountain near the Dead Sea. Our instructor stopped the bus right at the inevitable gift shop where you could buy the inevitable T-shirts. Like an arresting police officer, he read us our options. "You can walk up a goat path to the top of the mountain. It takes about three hours.

The temperature at this moment is 105°F. You can take the cable car to the top. Or you can wait here in the bus."

The frightened kid and the mature adult start a fist-fight in my psyche.

"Stay here in the bus!" yells the kid.

"You did not come all the way to Israel to sit in the bus all day," says my adult.

"But it's blazing hot out there and besides that goat path is cut right into the edge of a cliff and you might look down and then forfeit your falafel."

"You could take the cable car," says my adult.

"You hate cable cars!" screams the kid.

I take a cable car. I let three cars go by before I screw up enough nerve, but I get on, and I stand in the very middle holding on to a pole, stare determinedly at the floor and concentrate on bowel and bladder control.

"Isn't that a great view of the Dead Sea," says one of my companions.

I don't answer. I am not viewing the Dead Sea. I'm busy impressing my finger prints into that steel pole. They are there to this day. Two sets on two cars, because I had to come back down again. Go to Israel and check it out.

Acrophobia is the silliest of all diseases. I was more likely to be raped by a nun in Jerusalem than have a mishap on a cable car. But my stomach knew those cables always broke, every single time – any facts in my head notwithstanding.

My friend Stu, who flies small planes for fun, explains to me how airplanes are safer than cars. I know that. Who can argue with facts? Then he says, "Let me take you up for a spin, sometime," and I have to tell him, "Stu, facts have nothing to do with it. Perceptions are reality, and my perception is that airplanes, especially small airplanes, have fatal crashes on 120 percent of their flights, so thank you very much but I am staying here."

Our perceptions, not facts, are our reality. Our perceptions keep us from living a whole bunch of life, of doing things, accomplishing stuff, from having fun.

We want to do the dance of life but we keep watching our feet.

When You Gotta Go

"When you gotta go, you gotta go. If you don't go when you gotta go, when you get there, you'll find you've gone."

Any male past 50 will tell you the absolute truth of that statement. And while women (especially those who have been pregnant) may understand the inconvenience of a rebellious bladder, women hardly ever understand the symbolism – the deep and hidden meaning of it all. You see, almost everything a male person is and does and wants to be is symbolized by the silliest looking organ ever created.

Yes, this is a guy thing, but try to understand. It sounds ridiculous and silly because it is. We can't help it.

Male bonding and male competition begins when groups of small boys practice communal peeing, standing shoulder to shoulder to see who can pee the farthest and longest. Soon, target practice gets into it, to see who can hit a leaf or twig five feet away. It is very hard for a male to explain why this is important, but every male understands that it is.

I grew up in the cold winters of Manitoba where snow banks were autographed by young boys practicing "peemanship," urinating their names in the snow. At 40 below, and a wind-chill of another 40 degrees, the exercise posed something of a threat to one's budding masculinity.

Boys who go camping know and cherish the male ritual of standing in a circle around the bonfire. It happens last thing at night, just before bed, and if there were any females present, they have been sent off. In a great hissing ceremony they douse the campfire. Fire spits and coals pop when doused with urine, so care and agility are essential to this masculine bonding ritual.

It's the community this forms, the *gemeinshaft* that happens – something women seldom understand. Only a real *mensch* like Garrison Keillor could have written...

> *...of course for men it's much more grand*
> *women sit or squat:*
> *we stand*
> *and hold the fellow in our hand...*

I have an e-mail note from a friend who writes about his experience running the marathon: "It's a mass male territorial ritual. The New York Marathon boasts of 'the world's longest urinal!' The pre-race piss is unconfined. My running partner and I stand packed shoulder-to-shoulder with ten-thousand runners and empty our bladders on the pavement."

There's something deeply primitive about it all. On a photographic expedition near Banff a few years ago, we were concerned about bears raiding our supplies. Our guide instructed us to urinate at six-foot intervals in a circle around the packs. But only the men in the group. Female urine, he explained, doesn't do it.

It worked. The bears stayed away.

I remember wondering if primitive human males marked their territory the way male bears and dogs do. Is there something buried deep in the recesses of our psyche that tells us, "This is not just emptying your bladder, son. This is identifying who you are, marking your turf, protecting your harem."

I know. This is starting to sound really sexist. That's because it is. Let's face it, our history, our heritage, our traditions, maybe even our genes are full of sexism. Even our religion.

The patriarchs in the Hebrew Bible were obsessed with the circumcision ritual. There are over 100 references in the Bible to circumcision, the cutting of the foreskin, thus marking the man's covenant with God.

A couple of years ago I was telling the saga of King David to a group of men at a conference. When I told the part where David collects 200 foreskins to pay for his bride, I noticed that every one of the men in the audience crossed their legs. And every one of them looked as if he wanted to be somewhere else.

Let's face it, the guys at that conference, like the guys in the Bible, have some pretty strong instincts related to the old "family jewels." So it is no surprise that as we males move into the second half century of life, and things don't always work the way they used to, we start to worry about that part of ourselves.

And a visit to the doctor for the annual check up only deepens the concern. The doc seems to have an inordinate amount of concern for a male's plumbing. "How's the waterworks?" my doctor asks cheerfully. And he doesn't take my word for it. He subjects me to the most excruciatingly uncomfortable examination you can imagine – one that is simply too embarrassing to describe.

Of course, the water pressure is one of the first things to go, so that peeing out a campfire gets to be dangerous. Even the traditional male prerogative of stepping behind a convenient tree doesn't work anymore because it splashes on your shoes. As for writing your name in the snow, you could only do that if you were a very skilled line dancer.

Last week, flying home from Calgary, I was on one of those little egg beaters they fly in and out of our small airport. Nature called, as nature always does, just as the steward was smiling his way up and down the aisle with his cart of plastic food. When the aisle finally cleared, I almost stepped on the lap of the woman sitting next to me in my hurry to get to the bif. And when I got there, the plane hit an air pocket and...nothing. Zip. Then the plane hit another large air pocket, and not only did I lose the possibility, I lost the sense of urgency. And since the "return to your seats" sign was on, I headed back, climbed over the woman in the aisle seat for a second time and strapped myself in.

Bingo! Bladder bells ringing! But by this time we had begun our descent to the airport, and there was nothing to do but concentrate.

CONCENTRATE!!!!

When the plane finally stopped and the door was opened, I set a new world record for the 100 yard dash to the biffy in the terminal, only to stand there again. And wait. And wait.

It's not easy being male. (I'm sure it isn't easy being female either, but I haven't had much experience at that.)

We men are cursed by our own fixation on that flabby little tassel that has, it seems, a mind of its own and is determined to shatter, in the bedroom or the lavatory, that tiny, fragile bit of self-esteem we manage to bring into our dotage.

Yes, I know. This is a guy thing and it is ridiculous.

Try to understand.

And please, try not to laugh.

Grow Old along with Me

Peanut Butter and Jam

Savoir-faire.

I had to look those words up because not only do I not have it, I wasn't even sure how to spell it.

A few years ago, I was the guest of some eminent publishers in Ottawa. They were both francophone Canadians, and they took me to an elegant country club. On the white linen table cloth they had, count 'em, ten pieces of silverware at each place setting. Right away, I knew I was out of my depth. The last time I saw that many instruments was on a tray at the dentist's.

The waiter handed me a menu, not a word of which was in English. Nor did I recognize a single dish.

"Since you obviously dine here frequently and since my tastes are quite catholic," I said with considerable *élan*, "why don't you order for me." (*Élan* seemed like the appropriate word here, though I'm not sure if it means "cool" or is something you rub on sore muscles.)

My host smiled. Did I detect some condescension? "And do you have preferences in wines?" he asked.

"White," I said, and I wished my voice didn't sound quite so squeaky.

Just the flicker of an expression crossed his impassive Gaelic face, but I saw it. He quite clearly had me pegged as a flat-footed nerd from Plum Coulee who had never eaten in any restaurant more elegant than McDonalds. He was wrong. I actually grew up four miles from Plum Coulee.

In the town of Horndean, it was. Horndean had one school, one grain elevator, and not much else. But it had space where kids could run and romp and sit under a poplar tree and eat peanut butter and jam sandwiches for lunch.

To this day I feel most comfortable eating with kids. "What's your favorite food?" they want to know.

"Peanut butter!" I can declare with total honesty. "Peanut butter and jam sandwiches, with the peanut butter and the jam real thick so it squishes out the side when you bite it."

"Right on!" they yell, and we have instant solidarity.

Did you know there is an international organization known as the Adult Peanut Butter Lovers Fan Club. And they even have their own newsletter called *Spread the News*. They have 60,000 members and they had a conference in Arizona where 850 people went to talk about peanut butter and, best of all, eat things made with peanut butter. Peanut butter pizza, black bean and peanut butter burritos, beef kebabs with ginger peanut sauce, and peanut butter cheesecake.

The peanut butter cheesecake sounds good, but I prefer peanut butter and jam. I know of some folks who eat peanut butter and olives, and my dad once made a peanut butter and sliced raw onion sandwich. But then dad would eat raw onions with anything.

A peanut butter and jam sandwich, is after all, a complete and full meal if you put it on whole wheat bread. There's protein in the peanuts. You have whole grains in the bread which are supposed to be good for fiber or something. And fruit. In the jam. And sugar in the jam too. You need sugar for energy. So you could eat peanut butter and jam sandwiches every meal of your life and stay strong and healthy. (Go ahead, tell your mom you read that in a book, so it must be true.)

I have a peanut butter and jam sandwich every morning for breakfast just to start my day right, but sometimes, when I go on trips somewhere, I have to go for weeks without any. Like cigarettes, the dependency is as much psychological as physical. It's not that I wake up in the middle of the night in a cold sweat but I do find myself kind of lonely and I know I would feel better if I could only have a peanut butter and jam sandwich. It's a much harder addiction to handle, because you can send a cab driver out in the middle of the night to get you smokes or booze, but what do you do when you are by yourself in a hotel room and you crave a peanut butter sandwich at 3:00 in the morning?

I have spent most of my life knowing, deep in my anxiety-ridden psyche, that I should be far more sophisticated than I am, and that grown men are not supposed to like peanut butter and jam sandwiches. I should develop whatever *savoir-faire* is, and I should not be spooked by ten pieces of silverware on the table or a cloth napkin folded to look like a paper airplane. I should know there are more kinds of wine than red and white and at least be able to name one or two even if I can't tell the difference.

But damn it! Life is too short for that! Bev has a T-shirt that says, "When I'm an old woman, I shall wear purple." It's the first line of a marvelous poem – a liberation manifesto saying that as you get older, if you are lucky, you begin living by your own agenda, not someone else's. If you feel like wearing a purple sweater over clashing bright green slacks, you will darn well wear that. Bev doesn't particularly like purple, but she wears the T-shirt a lot.

If I ever get to a restaurant with ten pieces of silverware again, maybe what I'll do is make a virtue out of necessity (like in the matter of the red suspenders) and blab something real loud about, "Heck, down in Horndean all we used was a table spoon sharpened on one side. You folks here got some kinda disability you need all this here hardware?"

Then, when they bring the menu, I'll order me a peanut butter sandwich. In French, if I can manage it.

Of course, by the time we get to looking at the menu, I may be at the table all by myself, so it won't be half as much fun. I better fake the *savoir-faire* stuff just a little so I can keep a few friends and family to eat with. My daughter mutters, "You can dress 'em up but you can't take 'em out!" just often enough I think she may mean it.

Besides, being a really successful slob takes a lot of work and concentration and who needs more work and concentration? So maybe I'll be what I'm really good at. Inconsistent.

On the Back Porch of Life

This morning, Bev and I spotted the first clutch of ducklings in the slough-like creek or creek-like slough that runs past our back door.

Each year in early spring, all the breeding mallards move off to the marsh nearby, leaving a few infertile females and unattached males to patrol our creek. And we wait for the first mother duck to return from the marsh with her fuzzy little charges.

We try to count the babies, a dozen we figure, scurrying around mother, feeding on the algae that grows on the rocks. Seeing those tiny, fuzzy ducklings makes us feel warm and fuzzy inside, so we walk back to our house with the warmth of spring-time in our souls. All is well on this sun-drenched day in May.

This afternoon, sipping a cup of coffee on the back porch, I see the other side of that reality. I hear a great squawking and flapping of wings, and I see a weasel slip into the water and make off with one of the ducklings. Fifteen minutes later, the scene is repeated.

In each case, I run toward the creek to protect "my" charges, much too late of course. In each case, I feel anger and dismay. In each case, I feel rage at the four unattached drakes nearby who pay no attention to the "tragedy." In each case, I imagine an attitude of triumph, of glee, in the weasel as he scampers off with one of my beautiful little ducklings.

But with a second cup of coffee, some time to reflect. I watch mother duck and her smaller brood feed on the algae as if nothing at all had happened. If there is grief anywhere, *I* am the one feeling it. But why?

I grew up in the unsentimental world of mixed farming, where killing of animals was a necessary part of survival. I hunted rabbits and ducks for food. I have seen the brutish ways of the wild, and how the young and the weak are the first food of predators. The weakest must be first to die if the race is to be kept strong. Were it not for weasels and disease our creek would be polluted with mallards.

Feeding on my ducklings was as much survival for the weasel as escaping was a matter of survival for the ducklings. And why was I thinking of the weasel as "he"? I had no idea of its sex. Perhaps it too was a mother with a clutch of baby weasels to feed. Perhaps all that is irrelevant. All living things must feed to live.

Am I now a sentimental old man who wants the world to be full of sun-drenched creeks and fuzzy ducklings and no weasels? Am I an unnatural aberration, a freak that's kept alive by pension plans and modern medicine, when the real world is full of weasels that must kill to eat and mallards that must breed a dozen young so that two may live to breed again?

And are those of us who indulge ourselves in questions such as this a bunch of soft-headed fools sitting on the back porch of life, while the real world struggles its necessity behind us?

How Long Have I Got?

My dear adoring daughter cast her limpid gaze upon me. "You know, Dad," she said, "you'll look very distinguished when your hair has finished turning gray."

I began to wonder. Could I be getting on? Is it possible I'm not as young as I used to be? Quickly I checked my pulse. I couldn't find it. In a mild panic I phoned my friendly, neighborhood medic.

"Just give me the 10,000 mile checkup," I said very casually as I strolled into his office.

"You mean the 16,000 kilometer checkup," he corrected. Needless to say, between my doctor and myself there is a generation gap.

"Listen," I said. "The model you're looking at still runs on miles and gallons and yards and feet. This is a vintage body. A collector's item. They don't make our kind anymore."

He wasn't impressed. "Take your clothes off," he said laconically. Poking at the dear departed muscle in my middle he asked all sorts of personal and embarrassing questions. "How much exercise are you getting?"

"Well, I do manage to get up in the morning and drag myself to the breakfast table," I said. "And I do get to the table for lunch and also for supper. I even manage a bedtime snack most evenings. And I get a good workout jumping to conclusions."

He was under-whelmed.

Then he went to the deep-freeze and got out that little gadget with the tubes on the end that he sticks in his ears, and then plants the cold steel disc right on the place where your heart, until that moment, was beating. He listened in one place, then another and another, and even tried my back in half a dozen places.

I assume he heard something eventually, because when he told me to lie down on that rock-hard excuse for a bed, he didn't cover my face with a sheet.

"Have any trouble sleeping?"

"Well, I don't have trouble mornings. I usually have a nap before lunch. And I have a good nap in the middle of the afternoon. And I mostly fall asleep reading the paper after supper. But when I get to bed I often have a real problem getting to sleep."

He poked and prodded a few more places. "Does this hurt?"

"No, it tickles," I said, writhing in agony. Then he put on rubber gloves and checked my tonsils, though it did seem to me he was starting at the wrong end. "How's the plumbing?" he asked. I wondered for a moment if maybe the doctor was going to move up to a profession that paid a little more. "Well, I couldn't pee my name in the snow the way I used to as a boy, but things seem to go in one end and out the other according to plan."

Finally he stopped. Or maybe he gave up. "I have some bad news for you."

I braced myself. "Yes?"

"You've got an incurable disease."

"My God. What is it?"

"Life."

"Is it serious."

"Serious? It's terminal!"

At first I was going to laugh, but I wasn't sure he was being funny. "Is that all?"

"What else do you want?"

At home again, I looked in the mirror. "What else could I want?" I said to myself. "And yes, I *will* look very distinguished when I finish going gray."

If I don't go bald first.

A Damn Nuisance

On my 60th birthday, some friends gave me a cane. "Har! Har! You are over the hill, Ralphie boy." I laughed *with* them.

A year and a half later, I am walking with that cane. And I am madder than a junkyard dog. No, it's not what you think. I am not embarrassed at the idea of using a cane.

Well, only slightly embarrassed.

Okay, I'm embarrassed as hell, but that's not the main thing.

It slows me down. My knee slows me down. I hate it, not being able to walk as far and as much as I want.

The doc says it's osteoarthritis. So I went on the Internet and checked out osteoarthritis and found out far more than I wanted to know. Sixty percent of the folks my age have it. Is it comforting to know that? Osteoarthritis is a disease of aging, or a "degenerative" disease as they so delicately put it.

Age is a degenerative disease.

What degenerates mostly is the quality of the humor. Seniors cackle away at a whole collection of jokes along the line of,

"You know you are getting older when your idea of a good time is turning the electric blanket up to high." Or worse. "You know you're getting old when everything hurts, and what doesn't hurt, doesn't work." Or (and this is true) "Your children begin to look middle-aged."

I spent yesterday afternoon with my grandkids, Zoë and Jake who are at the other end of the age spectrum. The world is opening up to them. Zoë's main ambition in life now is to learn how to walk so she can get at all those neat things which are just out of reach. Jake is working on language, stringing all those complicated words together and making sentences and sense. He's a three-and-a half foot walking tape recorder. If you utter some inappropriate good old Anglo-Saxon expletive, you hear a small voice right beside you echoing it faithfully. Over and over in fact, until his mother (my daughter Kari) comes by and wants to know, "Where did he pick that up? Dad?"

Everything is up for children. New. They are gaining more and more new skills and knowledge and ability and the world is opening for them. But Kari is celebrating her 35th birthday this week and bemoaning the idea that, "This is officially the beginning of middle age." Piffle! Thirty-five is barely past pubescence.

For Jake and Zoë, the world is mostly opening up, but it is also shutting down. Already Jake is aware that there are things he is not allowed to do. He's having to give up the innocence of infancy. Soon he is going to have to face up to toilet training and give up the convenience of diapers. At the other end of the age spectrum, people sometimes find themselves giving up the convenience of continence and moving back to diapers.

Jake and Zoë will discover sexuality in a few years and will know the joy and the pain of all that. But then, gradually, it will dominate less and less of their consciousness and perhaps, like their granddad, they will find themselves like children again when sex seems less and less significant. Over the years, new horizons open up and old ones shut down, except it seems that somewhere in the middle years, there is a subtle shift and we face more shutting down and less opening up.

The cane is only a symbol. And I am railing against it to get myself in shape for a really king-sized snit when I'll have to give up my driver's license. Or something else that's really important to me.

I have a good friend who has lost his eyesight over the last few years. As far as I can tell, he's done it with grace and humor, though I have no idea if there was rebellion and anger raging in his soul. There should have been some.

The Welsh poet Dylan Thomas urged his father,

> *"Do not go gentle into that good night,*
> *Old age should burn and rave at close of day;*
> *Rage, rage, against the dying of the light."*

Except raging is hard work. It takes so much energy, and energy becomes more precious as you age. Raging doesn't accomplish anything anyway. Except burnout.

It's a skill we need to learn. Aging, I mean. Because more and more of us are doing it. There are more seniors now than there have ever been before, not only as a percentage of the population, but in actual numbers. And we're not prepared. We're not prepared as a society, where the governments are running scared of us because they know seniors have the political power and the smarts to use it. They also know we could suck the economy dry with our demands for pension and health benefits.

At a personal level, we're not prepared either. I went to school for years to get ready for a job. When I retire, they'll pat me on the head, wish me well, and throw me into the deep end of the pool. Most folks I know who have retired were not ready for it and are not doing it well. We need a post-grad degree in aging before we're allowed to get old.

I am at the beginning of the last third of my life. The actuarial tables tell me that I will probably live till my mid-80s in relative good health and then one of the biggies – heart or cancer – will take me to my grave quite quickly. But I will probably live that last third of my life in reasonable health because I am part of the first generation to know modern health care from cradle to grave.

My mom made us take a bath every week, whether we needed it or not. And she worried about things like nutrition. A tablespoon of cod-liver oil in the winter. Every day. And milk. We had to drink milk and eat vegetables. None of these concepts were there in her day. She learned them and applied them. Being raised by informed and health-conscious parents, plus modern medical benefits like beta blockers and Prozac will make it possible for me to live fairly well during the last third of my life.

Except for that knee. Except for the fact that I have started reading the obituaries because I find my friends there. So far, I've not read my own name there, which is reassuring. When I do, I will emulate Mark Twain and announce that "reports of my death have been exaggerated." There is a sense in which I've already seen my name there, because death is not a one-time event. It happens slowly over the years. Retirement is a small death, a *petit mort* as the French sometimes call an orgasm. When I leave my work, a hunk of me dies because I won't have a job to give my life focus; to give me identity and meaning, to provide much of my social life. This, by the way, is often more of a problem for men than for women.

We live in the city of Kelowna where many, many folks come to retire. The countryside is lovely and the climate (by Canadian standards) is moderate. There are many seniors here for whom retirement is wonderful. They are, quite literally, having the time of their lives and making a valuable contribution to our community and our world.

For others, perhaps most of them, retirement is hell. And the favorite way of dealing with that hell is hiding from it. Avoidance, the psychologists call it. Fill up your life with bingo and idle chatter and travel and lawn bowling and make sure you don't allow yourself time to entertain those ghosts that come in the middle of the night and tell you your life is over, you are not doing anything worthwhile, you are just taking up space. What you can't run away from, you drown in booze or anesthetize with prescription drugs.

Bev and I have an acquaintance of many years who had a heart attack a few years after he retired. Since that time, he has done nothing except focus on his heart. He goes walking, every day for several hours, with a look of grim determination on his face. If you talk to him, within two minutes he has the conversation focused on his heart. Everything he does, all his life energy, is focused on keeping that heart beating. He lives to keep his heart beating.

Frankly, if that is life, I don't want it.

Betty Friedan in an excellent book (*The Fountain of Age*) claims that those who live longest and well have several things going for them.

1) They have some reasonable control over their own lives. Nursing homes that control and regulate every aspect of the lives of their inmates are killers.

2) They have a community. They have friends and associates (and sometimes family) whom they enjoy being with and who enjoy being with them.

3) They have a vocation. By that I mean they have something to do that has meaning. They are making a contribution. Whether they get paid for this or not is irrelevant. Most are not. But the world is a better place because they are there, and they know it. They are not just taking up space.

When I talk about something worthwhile in your life – a vocation – I don't mean that you have to be elected "Citizen of the Year" or that you need to knock yourself out volunteering for everything. All I mean is that you try to give a little of yourself away each day. It may be as simple as phoning someone who is lonely, or dropping someone a note, or saying a prayer. Or asking the harried clergy or doctor who looks in on you, "How are *you*?" Nobody, unless they are unconscious, is so sick they cannot reach out to others in some small way.

Notice something missing from that list up there? Money. Yet every pre-retirement seminar or article that I've ever read talks almost entirely about money, as if having enough of it guaranteed a good retirement. I've seen wealthy retirees in Sun City, Arizona – snowbirds from Canada – struggling to fill up their time by making cutesy things out of pipe cleaners while they wait for happy hour. They've got money, but they haven't got a life.

Money is useful and important, but it ain't the main thing. Neither is physical health. We've all heard elderly folks say, "As long as I have my health..." Well, you can have all the parts ticking away wonderfully like a finely tuned BMW, but if that car has nobody in it and no place to go, it's really just a well-polished pile of junk. Healthy, wealthy seniors with nothing important to do and nobody to do it with are some of the most miserable and cranky old farts you'd ever have the displeasure of meeting. The only "good" news is that there is a whole service industry infra-structure springing up with a mission to convince these sorry old sots that they really are miserable and incompetent, and in the process relieve them of their money.

Author Gail Sheehy (*New Passages*) says this huge age bulge, which is happening now and is going to grow in the next 50 years, is the biggest social change since the opening of the American west. She may be getting just a bit overexcited, but it is a huge change for each of us personally and for our country. There needs to be a whole lot of systematic head scratching to figure out what all of this means.

In the meantime, I have this cane. And I have this problem of working out how I can live what the philosopher Paul Tournier called "the Sabbath of life," the time when we have the opportunity to more slowly, thoughtfully, reflect on our values and aspirations, and focus on that which is of central importance to us. Then we can make it our vocation to work toward that. We can focus our time and money on what is significant.

Life is a constant succession of giving things up. When Jake gives up diapers in favor of the toilet, he will give up some freedom. No longer can he pee on the run. He will need to stop what he is doing to take care of his bursting bladder, and that will not always be convenient.

I have to give up the idea of myself as a tireless walker. But I've noticed that when I carry my cane, people offer me a seat. And some of them are prepared to give me the status of the "elder," although that's a mighty precarious honor nowadays. A cane is a handy thing to point with, I've discovered, as long as you don't take out somebody's eye in the process.

Most of all, coming to terms with a cane frees me to set aside some of my "I don't need help from anyone" attitude, and realize my interdependence with others. I've got to work at building a community of friends. Maybe my cane will be a psychological signal to begin schooling myself toward retirement and discovering a vocation for the last third of my life. If my cane helps me to learn a few tricks to ease me into the Sabbath of my life, I can avoid becoming one of those cranky old farts I complain about.

In the meantime, it's a damn nuisance.

A Mere Pubescent 62

I make a lot of speeches.

It's not because I have important things to say, but I tell corny jokes and my fees are low, so I get to eat rubber chicken at Rotary Clubs and Lions meetings and casseroles at church potluck suppers.

The folks I meet at those events mostly complain about the same thing. "Look at all the gray heads," they moan. "Our membership is getting older and older!"

"Well, turn that problem into an opportunity," I say. Of course we are getting older. That's no surprise. There are far more of us who are now in that "senior" category, and this will increase in the next few years as the baby boomers reach for the Geritol.

But there is a radically different way in which we are *being* old. In our parents' day, debilitating illnesses would gradually sap strength and vigor so that "old and infirm" almost always went together. No more.

I am a mere, pubescent 62. Like the majority of people my age I have not had any serious illnesses. No heart problems. No

232 • Angels in Red Suspenders

cancer. I can expect to hit 80 before one or both of those gets me. Moreover I expect to do so in vigorous good health.

The problem is that after they hand us the gold watch and tell a bunch of lies about us at a retirement "do," they want us to disappear.

Who's "they"? Our colleagues at work, at the clubs, the church, the neighborhood. "You've had your turn. You've done your thing. We said 'thanks.' Now get lost! As far as anything important is concerned, you don't exist anymore. We'll make sure you are fed and clothed and warm and have your *Attends* changed, so don't bother us."

But just a damn minute!

We've been brainwashed into thinking that only the young are alive. Nothing has a future unless the youth are doing it. And there are just enough oldsters who retire from life as well as their jobs when they hit that magic age, to give that vicious rumor credibility.

But it's not true. Just because *some* folk turn into soggy meatloaf the day they retire doesn't mean all or even most of us do. I spent six decades getting to be as smart and as able as I am, and I am not about to roll over and play dead just because I have reached the official age of decrepitude.

My friend Glen and I used to go to a hockey game once a year whether we needed it or not. We particularly enjoyed the annual National Hockey League Oldtimers game against the local juniors: 18-22 year old "kids."

The old guys had lost their legs but they hadn't lost their smarts. They skated three steps for every mile the young guys went, but they always knew where their teammates were and where the puck was. The old fogies passed the puck while the young guys chased it.

Paul Henderson took a cross-ice pass, skated two steps toward the goal, leaned to his left, deeked that young goalie right out of his socks, and flipped the puck into the right side of the net. Beside me Glen snorted. "Age and duplicity beat youth and vigor every time."

We don't have the legs, the stamina, the energy, the bounce we had once. I tell my son I can do everything he does, I just can't do it as often. The recycling time is longer, but we still know the moves. The last thing to go is usually the brain.

On top of that, many of us have developed (maybe out of necessity) a healthy sense of humor and clear-eyed perspective about what is important and what is not.

It's called wisdom.

So I tell the Rotarians or the Lions or the church group, "The solution to the problems of your organization is under your nose. It's called 'gray power.' Me and my gray-haired friends could set your club or your organization back on its hind legs. We have more know-how (and just incidentally, more money) than any other age group."

Think gray.

We blue-haired biddies and cranky old farts are probably your greatest asset.

Old Dog, New Tricks

"You will be sick tomorrow if you don't stop this." So, I tried to stop it, but of course I couldn't, and yes I was sick the next day.

I was lying on my back staring at the ceiling of a monastery near Jerusalem. "What is a small-town Protestant Canadian boy doing in a Catholic monastery in Jerusalem?" I kept asking myself.

There I was, among a group of about 30 Roman Catholic priests at a Franciscan monastery in Jerusalem taking graduate courses in biblical archaeology. Not only that, I was the oldest of

234 • Angels in Red Suspenders

the whole lot, with the exception of one priest in his 80s who was fit and lively and constantly let you know it.

Trying to be optimistic, I told myself, "Well, you survived the first day." This was after traveling 32 hours from my home in western Canada to Jerusalem, and arriving at the monastery in the late evening totally strung out and zonked. My doctor had given me a sleeping pill for just this occasion, so I took it and was comatose for about 12 hours. That helped.

But the next day we were up at 7:00, on the bus by 8:00, and spent the day in the blazing sun at the Herodion, a luxury condo King Herod built about 2,000 years ago. It was exciting. It was wonderful. I took dozens of pictures and a whole notebook full of notes. Then we came back to the monastery, had a quick supper, and spent the evening in an orientation session.

Now it was midnight, and I was in trouble. All my childhood anxiety tapes were blaring in my head. Why had I not taken the option of auditing the course? Who needs academic credit when you are 60? How am I going to handle six weeks in the blazing sun every day? I'll wind up with a permanent headache. I can't keep up with these "kids" many of whom have Ph.D.s.

I began to fantasize how I might just leave a note for the course director, sneak out to a nice air-conditioned hotel somewhere, and read books for six weeks. Then I could go home on schedule and lie through my teeth about the great time I had in Israel.

I must have slept, because the next thing I knew the alarm was clattering and I stood up for ten seconds before a pounding migraine knocked me flat on my backside. I was sick, as predicted. My migraines usually last two or three days and find me on my back in bed with an ice-pack on my head. Where do I find ice in a monastery? Do Franciscan monks enjoy the occasional Scotch on the rocks? Then I remembered the wonderful medical breakthrough – a new pill my doctor had prescribed. Half an hour later, the headache was gone, but not the anxiety or the exhaustion.

Misery loves bedfellows, and I found them around the breakfast table. Every one of those priests was looking as if he had just been dragged through a knothole. Every one of them was complaining of tension and fatigue and exhaustion. Everyone, except a five-foot nun who looked happy and cheerful and fresh. I disliked her instantly.

"We are not going anywhere today," announced our course director. Cheers all around. "Yesterday was a taste of what this course is going to be like. Today we talk about how to survive it."

Lots of practical stuff that day about wearing hats and using sun-blocker and about Israeli currency and customs. I can only remember two things.

Dehydration will get you every time. If you wait till you feel thirsty before you drink water, it is too late. Have a bottle in your hand all the time, and take a little nip every five or ten minutes, whether you are thirsty or not. Stay away from the booze and the pop and the coffee. Just drink water.

Okay, says I to myself, but that presents a problem. If I drink that much water, I will be widdling like a nervous race horse. "Are there lots of washrooms around?" I asked our course director. "No," he said. "Hardly any. Go before you leave in the morning and then breathe deeply till you get home at night."

I was sitting beside the cheerful nun. She muttered a word I didn't know was in a nun's vocabulary. "I won't make it," she said.

"Neither will I."

"Well," she whispered to me brightly, "This may be a new experience for the Reverend Fathers, but they may well see Sr. Irene hoist her skirts and squat right there for all of them to see." Sr. Irene and I were good friends for the rest of the course.

It turned out not to be a problem. Sr. Irene and I limited ourselves to half a cup of coffee in the morning. We nipped at our bottles, as per instructions all day, but the water never got down to our bladders. We sweat it out, but the climate was so hot and dry our skin never got wet. The problem was no problem, but you do want to have a shower before you head for supper.

There was a second thing I learned.

Don't sweat the study stuff. That took a bit longer.

Maybe I should have audited the course, but I was cranky enough to say, "Hell, no. If I am going to do this, I am going to do it right." That was really easy to say six weeks before the trip began while I was sitting with a glass of wine in my easychair back home in Canada.

Except for that geriatric Franciscan, I was the oldest person on the course. It had been years since I did formal study. I had forgotten how to read the impenetrable prose of the scholars or how to write an academic paper. Actually I never knew how in the first place.

The young priests took far better notes, and generally had far better study habits than I did. In fact, I stopped taking notes altogether and concentrated on looking and listening and experiencing.

But I knew how to listen more effectively than my younger classmates. I also had far more general information, more life experience, more ability to separate the significant from the trivial than they did. They gathered more information but I *learned* more and found myself excited by what I was experiencing.

And guess what? This old curmudgeon aced both courses!

Who says old dogs can't learn new tricks?

Live Until We Die

Nothing like death to focus your living. That's what Bob Love did when he leaned over to Bev and me and said, "Live now!"

Bob used to be our family doctor, but by this time he had been promoted to the category of "old friend" and was specializing in cancer treatment.

Bev's Dad had just died. He had worked hard. Saved all his money. He and Madeline (his wife) bought a plot of land but the house they hoped to build never got beyond the drawings that cluttered the coffee table.

"Don't postpone your living," Bob pleaded with us. "I see people do that over and over. They postpone everything until some future date, when they'll retire or when they'll have enough money or something. But they never get to do it. *They never get to do it.*" Bob shook his head sadly. "So live *now!*"

I am now just about the age Bev's dad was when he died. Suddenly I am remembering Bob's words and wondering, what kind of living?

Bev and I had a great time last winter in Arizona. Bev lost an argument with a cactus plant and we found some narrow mountain roads that scared the daylights out of me. But mostly, we had a good time being tourists in Arizona.

It also gave us a good chance to watch the snowbirds – the "six-'n-sixers" who winter down there every year. Some are living healthily and happily and creatively. But others move around with a quiet desperation – a grim determination to keep busy, doing something, anything, just to keep from thinking about that terrible terminal illness which is lurking right around the corner. They spend the mornings making cute crafts out of toilet paper rolls, the afternoons sitting in the pool with their hats on, and their evenings drinking too much. Their entire focus is on themselves.

But why am I being so superior?

Get real, Ralph! A major social activity, once you hit 50, is going to the funerals of friends and business associates and relatives. Sometimes siblings. Like everyone else my age, I've had my health scare. It was a swollen lymph node and the time between the doctor noticing it, and the operation to remove it, was a small taste of hell.

It was a major shock to me when I sat at my brother's bedside and held his hand while he died. I grieved the loss of a brother, yes, but it was more. His death was a signal. This is *my* generation. My brother was one of "us kids."

Now it's my turn, and I am just as scared as those folks in Arizona.

I want to run. I do that well. I've been practicing all my life running away from problems.

Except this "problem" can run faster than I. My own mortality keeps whacking me on the snoot. "I have to sit down to pee," I tell the doctor, in the same tone of voice I might confess to having an affair with a hippopotamus. My body keeps sending me signals and I try as hard as I can to pay no attention. I run.

One of the ways I run is to read books. As long as I am reading stuff (I call it "research") I don't have to actually *do* anything. But the book I am reading, *The Fountain of Age* by Betty Friedan, tells me (among more things on aging than I really want to know) that studying the subject of aging is the best thing I can do. On the face of it, that sounds like a recipe for hypochondria. Read on.

Remember Betty Friedan? Friedan was one of those delightfully annoying women who kick-started the feminist movement a few decades back (*Feminine Mystique*). Now she's writing about old farts and blue-haired biddies and telling us the fundamental problem for seniors is the same problem women faced a few decades back. Turns out she is writing about the same thing that Bob Love was talking about.

Who is in charge of your life?

Friedan tells about some researchers who collared a bunch of old geezers and asked them to help on a program of research into aging. These geriatric gentlemen got so much into the research – so deeply into the issues of aging – they forgot to die on schedule. Long after all the actuarial charts said they should have been pushing up daisies, these seniors were still pushing up new insights and ideas. Why quit when you're having fun?

It was a clue.

Friedan says the women who grabbed hold of their own destinies on the wave of the feminist movement had surprises for the experts on aging too. They breezed through menopause, forgetting completely they were supposed to be tied up in emotional knots because of it. As for the "empty nest syndrome," it was as if somebody gave them the keys to the cage.

These same women, moving into "retirement," are going back to school, starting new careers, doing things they've wanted to do since their first pregnancy.

Most men, on the other hand, struggle and fuss until they get the gold watch and the pension cheque. Then they come home, turn on the TV, and die within a few years. "Why is it," asks Friedan, "that men die so much younger than the women?" Women are supposed to be the "weaker sex," remember?

The gerontologists who do long and boring studies into aging don't have a lot of clues, for the most part. They tend to look at the people warehoused in retirement homes, the veterans hospitals, the senior citizens' villas. They study those good old boys who do exactly as they are told, which includes dying on schedule.

But take a look at the exceptions. What happens if you study the feisty elders who are not as "good" and who will not do as they are told and who take charge of their own destinies – who will not let themselves be committed to a nursing home? What can you learn from the sages who live until they die?

Surprise!

Their life-spans begin to look a lot more like their sisters (or wives) and what is far more important, they do not turn into the doddering dim-wits you see portrayed on TV. Like old wine, they get better. They can't run as fast as their younger brothers, but they can think better. They lose almost nothing in terms of factual memory, and gain a whole bunch in the much neglected area called "wisdom." The more they are in charge of themselves, the more they take on challenges and do things they feel are important, the healthier and happier they are, and the longer they live.

So having heard Bob Love and Betty Friedan, the first thing I need to do is have a heart-to-heart with Bev, and what I need to say would go something like this.

Once you were my blushing bride and I was your blushing groom. Neither of us are blushing anymore, but we still love each other and, which is more important, we like each other. So, "grow old along with me," to quote the poet. "The best is yet to be." But for that best to be, we need to be realistic about the problems and possibilities during these, our senior years.

We've got to confront our aging. There are realities we've got to face. I can no longer pee in the woods without wetting my shoes, so let's install a port-a-pottie in the minivan. Let's not be secretive or coy about our problems, but let's joke about them with our friends. We can exorcise the demon by laughing at it.

We need to talk, eyeball to eyeball, about what accommodations you need and I need. Then we shall have a good laugh, and maybe a bit of a cry, do what needs to be done, and move on to the next problem.

How are we going to take charge of our lives? How are we going to make sure that we hear God's call to be who we are, to live significantly and fully, to make our lives (whatever there is left of them) mean something? We probably each have about 20 years of fruitful, productive life. In that time, we can make a difference to this hurting world.

But let's not forget that it's important we continue to embarrass our children by enjoying every minute of our lives as fully as possible. And we must take lots of time to delight in our grandchildren. It's our duty.

Let's pay attention to Bob and Betty. Let's live fully now, and make sure we're in charge of us.

To Make Things Beautiful

"Look at the blue in those tiny petals," she squealed. "It is just so lovely."

And it was. At least, after she showed it to us and her enthusiasm infected us. We wouldn't have seen the flower without her to notice it for us.

This was a tour group out of Valdez, Alaska. "Tide to Tundra" it was called, and two young women took a dozen tourists trundling in a school bus up the mountainside through Keystone Pass and up above the tree line. One of the women called the tundra "my back yard," and bounced up a hillside to bring back a small bouquet of wildflowers. She knew their names, she knew their attributes, and she very clearly loved them. And for that moment, she helped us love them too.

The philosopher's question. That flower with the tiny, blue petals. Was it beautiful before our tour guide noticed it? Up on that windswept tundra, clods like me would walk right over such an insignificant flower. We step on it and kill it. But she saw it and pronounced it beautiful, and thus, I think, completed God's creation.

In the old, old creation legend in the Bible, God creates everything that is, and then says, "Behold, it is very good." But not until young women notice small blue flowers and marvel at their beauty is God's creation fulfilled. Beauty exists only in the eye of the beholder.

God made this universe, but only God's creatures can make it beautiful.

I sit across the table from my friend, Jim Taylor. I'm reflecting on the story of the flower, and of other beauty Bev and I have seen on our just-completed trip into Alaska. "It's my job, as your friend, to make you beautiful, Jim," I say.

"Now that's a stretch!" Jim grins.

Which is true. Neither Jim nor I have been asked to pose (with or without clothes) for any magazines lately. Or ever, for that matter. We may have some redeeming qualities which we manage to sublimate quite well, but it's been awhile since anyone described either one of us as "beautiful."

But still. It is our job as friends to make each other beautiful. Who but friends could see behind the grizzled exterior of two geriatric curmudgeons? Who but longtime friends can know the gentleness behind the gruffness? There is nothing objective, rational, or analytical about such seeing, any more than my appreciation of that little blue flower was objective, rational, or analytical.

God created our world. That includes our friends. Our family. Tiny blue flowers. Tour group leaders. Aging friends. Our job is to recognize their beauty – to love it, and whenever possible, proclaim it.

The Time of Our Lives

Peeing Your Pants

Derek and I were friends.

Friends under some strange circumstances, but friends. He was about four and I was about 40.

Derek attended the nursery school just down the hall from where I had my office in a church basement. This was a number of years and a world of innocence ago when these things could happen without anyone getting twitchy.

One day, when I was using one of the cubicles for its appointed purpose in the bathroom that my office shared with the nursery school, I heard the outer door open but paid no attention till a small face peered under the door at me.

"Hi!" I said.

The face disappeared, I heard the door slam, and a small voice yelling, "Teacher! Teacher!" Then adult footsteps approaching somewhat hurriedly, the door opening and a small, anxious voice saying, "Teacher, there's a man in there!"

"Yes, Derek." I could hear the embarrassment in her voice. "That's all right." And then, apparently directed at me in the cubicle, "I'm so sorry!"

This situation, I decided, needed to be addressed. The nursery school teacher's face went beet red when I introduced myself as "the guy in the bathroom." She started to apologize but I interrupted.

"Look, I'm a family man. I have kids of my own, so have a good laugh and don't worry about it. But I think you should introduce me to Derek." Which she did, and I explained to my new friend that I used the same bathroom. Derek wanted to know what I was doing in there, and what followed was a quick lesson about subjects that should have been taught at home by a father. But I learned later that Derek didn't have a father at home.

Derek had almost mastered the intricacies of going to the bathroom, but he didn't have his timing down quite right. The next time I met Derek, he was in the bathroom, his pants were down around his ankles and he had tears in his eyes.

"What's the matter?" I asked. It was a dumb question. I could easily see what the matter was.

"I peed my pants," said Derek.

"That's okay," I said. "I'll get you some dry ones from the teacher."

"Big boys don't pee their pants," he said, sounding very angry at himself.

"Sure they do," I said. "Metaphorically speaking."

"I don't know what that means," said Derek. I wasn't sure I did either.

"Well," I said, "you really tried hard to get to the bathroom on time, but even though you tried, you still did what you didn't want to do. Big people try very hard to do the right things too, but often, even when they try hard, they mess up. Do you understand that?"

"No," said Derek, in no mood for a philosophical discussion. He wanted some dry pants, which I put on him along with a few more reassuring words.

Derek didn't know it, but he and I are soul-mates. I understand his problems completely. I've been there.

When you think about it, that's what the spiritual life is all about. It's about people who wet their pants, and about a God who dries them off, cleans them up, gives them a hug, and sends them back to nursery school to keep on learning about life.

The Inner Meaning of Turkeys

There's an old saying that in the land of the blind, the one-eyed person will rule.

Not so.

In the land of the blind, the one-eyed person will be pronounced mad. Bonkers. El nutso. The one-eyed person might be tossed in jail or executed as a dangerous revolutionary.

In the land of the blind, the one-eyed person would be aware of things nobody else knew about, and if that person spoke publicly about that, the blind folks would send for the nice men to come and keep our one-eyed friend well sedated in a home with padded walls.

Human beings have a wonderful way of recognizing only their own reality. If your reality doesn't match mine, *you* must be wonky. If you see something I don't see, *you* are nuts.

Next time you have a turkey for dinner, reflect on the inner meaning of that much maligned bird – shamelessly splayed in boorish nakedness on your table.

As a boy, I would watch the turkeys on our farm. I can tell you with absolute certainty that the turkey's reputation for stupidity is well-deserved. When a hawk or a sparrow or an airplane flies overhead, they turn their heads to one side looking up, first with one eye, then the other. This is just before they all stampede into the barn trampling and maiming each other in the process.

Turkeys can only see out of one eye at a time. That's true of many birds and animals. But most human folks can see out of both eyes, together. That's why we are eating turkeys and turkeys are not eating us.

Play a little game with yourself. Hold up a finger about a foot away from the end of your nose. If your nose is as large as mine, that'll be almost at arm's length. Close one eye, then the other, blink them back and forth while looking at your finger. The finger seems to move. Your two eyes don't see the same thing, but if you look with both eyes, the brain takes the two images, puts them together, and figures out how far away that finger is.

Or you can play a dumb parlor game based on the premise that people enjoy making themselves and others look ridiculous. Choose a victim, preferably someone who hates parlor games. Have the victim cover one eye. Then hold your finger about three feet in front of the victim's nose. Ask the victim to touch the tip of your finger, coming at it from the side.

It's called binocular vision. Or stereoscopic vision. Depth perception. Humans have it. Turkeys don't. It gives us quite an advantage over turkeys.

Maybe that's why we think we are smarter than turkeys, though I doubt the turkeys think so. Any half-witted turkey knows that when there's something flying around up there, you can't tell if it's a sparrow or a hawk or an airplane. Not having binocular vision, turkeys are convinced nobody else can either. Humans are operating under a pious delusion. Turkeys also know that you can't tell how far away it – whatever "it" is – might be. So only one response is appropriate...

Panic!

Humans don't need to panic. We can tell how far away that flying thing is, and therefore we have an idea whether panic is the best response.

Humans know another neat trick. We can get a couple of humans looking up there. We get four eyes on the job. Then we can tell each other what we see.

Just as two eyes see different things, two people looking at the same thing see two slightly different things. And three people see three different things. And four people see four different things. (I could go on, but I think you've got the idea.)

I do this with children sometimes. I ask one child to stand in front of me, and the other to stand behind me. "What do you see?" I ask.

"A bald spot," says one.

"A big nose," says the other.

"So who is right?" I ask.

"We're both right." And that's right. But it takes two people seeing different things to get a complete picture. Stereoscopic experiences. As somebody once said, "None of us is as smart as all of us."

There are no two people in the world who are identical. Not even identical twins are totally identical. Every single one of us is different. It would have been a lot easier for the Creator to have used just one cookie cutter and made us all the same. But no. Every one of us is different. There's got to be a reason.

I thought about that over supper today, because we were eating with a couple who are "born-again" Christians from a Bible church that "preaches salvation." Their language, their way of expressing their faith is not the same as mine, coming as I do from a liberal, social-justice orientation.

Who's right? We both are. So is the young aboriginal American who danced his spirituality for us not long ago in Juneau, Alaska. Or the Buddhist or the Sikh or the Moslem or the Jew. All of them may be right.

Turkeys would find that a hard concept, but it should be easy for humans. Unfortunately, it isn't.

Turkeys have a brain the size of my thumbnail, monocular vision, and they can't talk. Humans are not as perceptually challenged as turkeys and should know that two realities can be totally different, and they can both be true. You and I can disagree and we might both be right. Yes, it is possible.

Now, carry that idea one huge step forward.

We humans can see reality, not only from the people perspective, but from God's perspective as well. Over the centuries, humanity has been blessed by saints and seers and shamans and prophets and messiahs who have come and shared their vision of God with us. Hearing their stories and singing their songs helps us see a whole new dimension to life. Our spirituality, our faith gives us a stereoscopic vision that adds depth and dimension to existence and gives life a fullness and a freedom we could never imagine without it.

Our faith perspective, whatever that is, helps us be aware of good and evil, beauty and joy, laughter and the depth of sorrow. We see injustice. We see hope.

Of course it's dangerous. The spiritual turkeys of the world think we're mad. They think we're dangerous. How can they possibly believe our vision when they can't see it?

In this land of one-eyed people who can't see much in life beyond scrambling up their own little ant hill, stereoscopic vision – the eyes of faith – can be dangerous to your health.

And wonderfully exciting.

The Chapel in the Washroom

My longtime friend Glen Baker held an important church office for awhile, and this got him traveling all over. Once, while visiting a small congregation in northern BC, he was invited to "dedicate" the new indoor bathroom that had just been installed. He agreed to do it following the main part of the program.

"But while that was going on," Glen recalls, "a toddler wandered through the bathroom door, which was standing open right behind the speaker. And in full view of everyone, baptized the facilities in a most appropriate manner."

"Glen," I asked, "Is there an appropriate prayer to bless a bathroom?"

"Well now, that's worth thinking about," said Glen.

Exactly. There should be. With the exception of the bedroom, there's no other room in the house that is more in need of God's blessing.

It is in the bathroom, after all, that we most often see the reality of who we are. We stand there, naked before the mirror and before God, with our pretensions lying in a heap, like our soiled and soggy clothes, on the floor. Before we join the folks in the living room, we can tighten the belt one notch, hitch up the bra another inch, powder the zit on the nose, comb the hair over the bald spot, or check our lipstick. But first, we have to confront the reality that we see in the mirror. For me, that is no great aesthetic joy. A Greek god I am not.

It's in the bathroom that we deal with the most basic necessities of life and with all the sounds and smells that go with it. It's in the bathroom that we kneel – face over toilet, head pounding and stomach heaving – and repent for the sins of the night before.

In the movie *Oh God*, the first appearance of God to John Denver is in the bathroom. "Don't worry. You don't need to be ashamed," says George Burns playing the part of God. "I know what you got." If God is anywhere, God is in the bathroom – an important theological concept!

A spiritual life worth having is not just for the special times. If it's only there for us when we're walking through the sun-drenched mountains with Julie Andrews singing, "The hills are alive..." it's not worth having. It's got to be there for the rotten times too, when you've lost your job or your partner or your self-respect or the doctor has just said you have breast or prostate cancer, or when you are just plain depressed or bored.

Spirituality needs to be there for the grundge times, the ordinary times, the day by day stuff. Getting the kids off to school or fixing the leak under the sink or realizing for the 400th time that Mr. or Miss Wonderful has zits on his/her buttocks.

God has got to be there in our bathroom with us, knowing everything we've got. Or not got. Our spirituality has to be there when we see our naked selves in the mirror, morning after morning, before we have time to clean ourselves up, before we can tuck in our tummies and brush away the dragon mouth. "Just as I am, without one plea," as the old hymn goes.

There should be a special blessing for bathrooms.

I learned about bathroom blessings the day I wandered the halls of an office building in lower Manhattan. I was there for a meeting, but the room was full of smoke and I could feel myself getting a migraine headache. It was a big meeting. They wouldn't miss me if I snuck out for awhile, because I knew that fresh air or sleep were the only possible cures.

I looked outside the window and realized that fresh air, in lower Manhattan, was as scarce as welfare moms on a cruise ship. So I headed for the men's biff, sat down in one of the cubicles, and used a technique I'd developed during years of singing in church choirs where you learn how to sleep sitting up, and with your eyes open, if necessary.

I had my snooze and got rid of my headache. But later on, over coffee during a break in the meeting, I was exchanging small talk with another man. "Y'know," he said. "I went into the can a few minutes ago. And there was a guy in the cubicle next to me. He was snoring."

He looked at me strangely when I laughed a little harder than he thought necessary. I never told him it was I who had been snoring. I was just thankful that even public buildings have private little chapels where millions of people have gone when there was nowhere else to be alone with their pain.

Sometimes the old biff is the only place you can go to wait for the Spirit to give you whatever you need to carry on.

On a cold winter day, I drove two hours in a rented car to make a speech. It was a big speech – an important speech. I arrived about 20 minutes before I was to stand up and do my thing. As usual, I went to place my text on the podium. It was not in my brief case. I searched frantically, everywhere, everything, the car, my pockets, my briefcase for the tenth time, but no speech.

I felt sick enough to throw up. Five minutes to show time, and I had nothing to say. Nothing! I retreated to a nearby bathroom, locked the door and wept. Then I prayed. Then I tried to make an outline on a paper towel. Except I couldn't read my normally terrible scrawl made worse by soft paper and written on my lap.

"All right, God. This is it. This speech is going to happen on pure adrenalin. Or faith. Or both."

Five minutes into it I realized, "I can do this! I've got the main points of this diatribe in my noggin." Ten minutes in, I began to relax a little. Twenty minutes in, I was having a good time seeing the response in faces, making the eye contact, responding to the puzzled looks, enjoying the smiles and the laughter. Thirty minutes, and I wound it up with a flourish, and got a standing "O".

I headed back to my chapel in the washroom, where I alternately cried and laughed, and the tears and the laughter were my prayer of thanks.

Yes, Glen. Bathroom chapels need a very special blessing.

A Package Deal

No one wants to be poor. There's no money in it.

A corollary would be – no one wants to suffer. It hurts.

We laugh at that because it is obvious. But the thing gets sick when we suggest, and we do, that no one should ever suffer or be in pain. I was told by a medical doctor once that his only real function was "to remove pain."

Maybe it can be argued that poverty can be eliminated. But pain? If some great savior could remove all pain from the world, would that be a good thing? If some medical genius invented the universal narcotic without side effects – the ultimate Prozac with which we would always feel good about everything – would we want it?

"I think, therefore I am." Descartes wrote.

Better still might be, "I feel, therefore I am." Or, "I hurt, therefore I am."

You've heard the story about the guy who got into his cups a bit much one night, and in a drunken stupor, wandered into a funeral home and passed out in a coffin. When he woke up the next morning, he looked around and thought, "I am in a coffin, therefore I must be dead. But if I am dead, why do I have a pounding headache and why do I have to go to the bathroom?"

I feel; I hurt, therefore I am.

Here's another one. I love, therefore I hurt. Sadly, the reverse (I hurt, therefore I love) doesn't follow.

"They shall laugh, but not all of their laughter. They shall cry, but not all of their tears," wrote the poet Kahlil Gibran in *The Prophet*. If you want to really live, he said over and over, jump into the deep end of the pool. Love people. Love them passionately and deeply. You will laugh and you will cry, and your laughter and tears will come from the same place in your soul.

Bev, my partner of almost 40 years, is clergy and has performed many weddings. In her address to the bridal couple she sometimes says, "You have promised to love each other 'for better or for worse.' Well, I can't promise that it'll get better than this. But it *will* get worse."

Bev knows from personal experience, living with me and our children these four decades, that the joy of loving anyone involves deep pain, disappointment, frustration and anger. The romantic love most couples feel during the wedding ceremony lasts a year or two. Then it changes into a different, deeper, more profound love or the marriage is over. It is the kind of love that knows both the tears and the laughter. It's the kind of love that demands a conscious choice.

That's true of parenting as well. It's easy to love a cuddly new baby, but that baby will become a nine-year-old, then a teenager, and will reject your love while needing it desperately. That sometimes takes a hard, very conscious decision. "I will love that kid of mine whether he/she wants me to or not."

It's true of friendship. Jim Taylor and I have been friends and colleagues for years. We've had to work at it. We meet once a week for lunch whenever we are both in town. Sometimes we argue and sometimes we're working through hard, personal stuff, and sometimes we tell the worst jokes you ever heard and sometimes we annoy the hell out of each other. We're both opinionated workaholics, and our friendship would never last if we didn't make it a choice. We've chosen friendship, not because it's easy, but because without it we are only half alive.

In the cartoon *Hi and Lois*, the eldest son is wailing away with his guitar, and the kid brother asks, "How can I become a singer like you." "You can only become a singer," says the older brother, "if you've really suffered." In the last frame, the kid brother is walking around looking desperately miserable. Lois is saying to Hi, "I don't know. He was quite cheerful this morning."

That cartoon is funny, because the humor touches a fundamental truth. You sing the song out of the pain. The joy of life is part of the pain of life. You cry for the loss of a loved one because you loved that person. We do not weep for those we have not loved.

If you want to live the full, abundant, meaningful life that sages and saints throughout the ages have promised, you must love passionately and work for the good of those you love, even, especially, when they have you climbing the walls. Unless we love passionately, we live only half a life.

But if we love deeply, we will get hurt.

Badly.

No exceptions.

Sorry about that. But the abundant life and suffering servanthood go together.

It's a package deal.

Survivors

In a campground last summer, I found a most unusual birch tree.

All the other trees were growing straight and tall, except this one. It jogged, about eight feet up. The trunk veered off to one side, then straight up again.

Some years ago, a much smaller birch tree must have been decapitated. With its top lopped off, the birch tree might have despaired and died. It might have turned into a neurotic, scraggly bush growing in every direction. But in my imagination, I could hear this birch tree say, "Well, if I can't grow here, I'll just move over a little and grow somewhere else."

I've been reading the story of Terry Waite, called *Taken on Trust* (Doubleday, 1993). I met Waite in 1983, at the meeting of the World Council of Churches in Vancouver, when he was envoy to the Archbishop of Canterbury. I was trying to get an interview with the Archbishop. Waite said "No," but then I found myself walking across the campus of the university with this man who was emerging as one of the remarkable figures of the world church. I felt dwarfed. He's 6 foot 6 with a frame to match. In the ten minutes of that walk, I found I really liked the man. There was no BS. He was real, and could be trusted. Either that, or a marvelous actor.

On a genuine, though perhaps misguided, mission to negotiate the release of hostages in Lebanon, Waite was taken hostage himself and spent almost four years in solitary confinement in a windowless prison where he couldn't stand up straight.

"I sat down and began to prepare myself for an ordeal," Waite writes. "First, I would strengthen my will by fasting. Secondly, I would make three resolutions to support me through whatever was to come: no regrets, no false sentimentality, no self-pity.

"Then I did what generations of prisoners have done before me. I stood up and, bending my head, I began walking round and round and round and round."

Waite was released, his faith stronger, his spirit triumphant. He was still growing, though not in the same place as when he entered that prison.

Terry Waite and my birch tree would have understood each other.

A Traditional Christmas Gift

Winter came in cold and early this year, and with it Bev's annual question. "What are we going to give the kids for Christmas?"

It's a necessary question but I never like it. Bev is the kind of person who likes to have things decided well ahead and I like deciding things at the last minute so you don't close your options till you have to. That's made our marriage interesting.

There's another reason I don't like the question and it's harder to explain. At the edge of the reason is the time-honored Christmas tradition of complaining about how commercialized it's all become and then buying just as much stuff as ever. Maybe more.

I get the impulse every Christmas to give lavish, expensive gifts. In fact, I'd like to do that any time of year, just on the spur of the moment, whenever I see something that fits somebody I particularly care about.

I'd also love to receive gifts like that but I almost never do. In spite of all my hints, Bev has never given me a bright red Alfa Romeo. Not even a pale pink Pinto.

Because we've chosen to live on very little cash, we budget our gift buying, just like everything else. Somehow that seems like a contradiction. Giving should not be budgeted. It should be wild and extravagant.

A gift should be rare. It should bring a surprised screech and exclamations of "Oh, you didn't! You shouldn't have!" And the proper response would be, "I know I shouldn't have. But I couldn't help it."

We don't do it that way. We plan our gifts and make sure one child gets about the same number and the same value of gifts as the other kids. And when I play "Santa" on Christmas morning, I space out the giving so that each of our kids and Bev gets gifts handed to them almost in turn.

Still, every Christmas, there's a wild child inside me that would like it to be totally spontaneous, extravagantly, impulsively giving and receiving.

Wouldn't that be wonderful?

No.

Because the best part, the hardest part, would be left out. That's the part where you make a commitment to love even at those times when loving is not easy. Especially at those times when loving is not easy. Loving the people in our own family is generally the hardest thing we ever do in our whole lives. I'm not talking about the Norman Rockwell kind of mush but the real love that happens when folks are hurting or messing up; when teenagers are acting out and folks are being unreasonable, stupid, cranky.

260 • Angels in Red Suspenders

The real gift is the careful, thoughtful struggle to do or give whatever fills the deepest need. If it is a thing, a tangible object, the gift is in the thoughtfulness and caring behind it, and the object is only a symbol of that caring. If there's no reality behind the symbol, it's meaningless and fraudulent.

With some of our family this Christmas, we've asked for something very special. "Don't give us a 'thing' we say, because we have far more things than we need. We don't have any more spaces to put any more things, and besides, we can go and buy whatever we need. Give us a piece of yourselves." We've asked for, and we propose to give, letters to those we love, with specific proposals and plans for getting together. "Our gift to you this Christmas," our letters will begin, "is that we are going to begin right now to plan a family get together. We are not just going to say, 'We should get together more often,' we are going to get on the phone before mid-January and start negotiating dates, places, etc. Because what we want for Christmas is more of you."

We had a gift like that last Christmas when we were given Zoë Rachel early in December. Imagine the gift of a grandchild. You can't do better than that.

Now what are we going to give Zoë? The grandparental juices flow in Bev and me as much as anyone, but the main gift we hope to give Zoë and her brother and her parents is us. Sounds a little pretentious, I know. But think about it. There's really nothing else we have to give them.

And this gift of self, this gift of presence, it turns out, is the most traditional of all Christmas gifts. This Christmas in our church we will read the story of the birth of Jesus, and hear how that baby was God's gift of presence. One of Jesus' names was "Emmanuel" which means, "God with us." And the story goes on about how that Emmanuel stayed with us and showed us, with an intensity that's hard to imagine, how much he loved us.

First God gave humanity the world. In other words, everything. Then God gave us God. Which is a wonderful solution to the gift giving problem. For the person who has everything – when you have nothing more you can give – give yourself. You can never be more generous than that.

So the Christmas idea Bev and I had turns out not to be original at all. Very traditional, in fact. But it's a gift that's far easier for me to write about than it is for me to do. I'm way better at the theory than the practice.

Some people won't like our gift idea. "Too damn cheap to buy a decent present," some will mutter. It's quite probable some will say, "The last thing we want is more of Milton around here." So it's not a gift we can give to everyone. Some want a gift you can take back to Sears and exchange the day after Christmas.

It may also turn out to be very, very expensive. That's a real risk.

But the older I get, and the more "stuff" I accumulate, the more that gift of self from the people I love will be at the very top of my wish list.

That's all I really need.

Shut Up! Sit Down! Row!

"I'm going to write a book called *The Adult Children of Parents*." That was a quip on the radio the other day by a woman who was sick of reading books with titles like, *Adult Children of Alcoholics* or *Adult Children of Codependents*. She was pointing to the obvious fact that every one of us comes from a dysfunctional family – that all of us carry a legacy of pain along with a legacy of hope. None of us had perfect parents. None of us were perfect children. All of us are human.

Neither the woman on the radio nor I (in quoting her) are in any way minimizing the soul-wracking pain suffered by many children at the hands of their parents. We are simply pointing out that all of us are, to a greater or lesser degree, codependent on our parents. On our politicians. Our teachers. Our clergy. And especially our spouses.

People are often unhealthily dependent on their doctors. The common term, "doctor's orders" is a handy way of avoiding responsibility for your own health. Doctors can't order anything. They can't even keep you in hospital against your will unless you are declared mentally incompetent or the police are keeping you there.

Some doctors foster that relationship – they try to appear omnicompetent. Frankly, if my doctor didn't quite often tell me that his diagnosis was an "educated guess" I'd change doctors. And I find it comforting that he often has to look things up.

There's been – there still is in many cases – a codependent relationship between the members of a church and its leadership. Clergy are often seen as a "father" figure who knows everything, who can fix everything, and who can stand up, face the culture, and say the words that make everything right again.

It doesn't work anymore. The wise old doctor, the all knowing preacher, the long-standing mayor or councilor – these folks may have existed once, though I hunch they've been "Norman Rockwelled" out of all reality. Now, when these kinds of folk stand up to speak, reporters stand around salivating, waiting for them to shoot themselves in the foot.

So the only alternative is for our leaders to sit down in the boat with the rest of the folks, grab an oar and say, "Okay friends. I don't know where the shore is either. So point the bow into the wind and row like crazy!"

Much the same thing is happening in families. I have fond memories of those few years when our children were very tiny, when I, as father, could do no wrong and was all wise and all powerful in their eyes. When they hurt, I could kiss it better.

It was a lovely time. But if it had continued, it would have become very sick. For parents, for leaders who insist on that kind of veneration, it degenerates into codependency. There's the dad, standing in the bow of the boat, lecturing at the waves while the boat sinks and everybody drowns.

Children need to grow up. "There's a statute of limitations on how long you can blame us for who you are," I say to my kids. "From here on, you take responsibility for your own life." I'd like to haul in every doctor, club leader, clergy and teacher they ever knew and have them say the same thing to every child they had in their care.

Family life, community life, is a scary business as we move into the third millennium. It would be nice if some strong daddy stood up and turned our struggle into a sunshiny cruise. I don't think that's likely to happen.

I have little patience with people who want to take us back to the days of my father when there were neat, packaged answers for all of life's questions – when we all assumed that "Father knows best," and that doctors and preachers had a special hot-line to heaven and therefore always and only spoke truth.

My response to them is simply, "Shut up! Sit down! Row!"

Everything Is Connected

Small leaks are connected to big repair bills.

I put a tin can to catch a small leak under the sink in the kitchen and emptied it once a day. When I remembered. Remembering was my job, because emptying that can had been declared (not by me) part of the dishwashing function, and my job was to wash the dishes.

Early one morning Bev went into the kitchen and took a skid on the water all over the linoleum. I was asleep, which is just as well because I hunch the exact words Bev used on that occasion (morning is not her best time) are better not reported. She retrieved the brimming can of water, walked into the bedroom where I was still sawing logs, said something impolite to wake me, and held the can of water exactly six inches over my nose while exacting a promise that I would fix that tap immediately, if not sooner.

Déjà vu.

Years earlier, in a small walk-up apartment in Winnipeg. I was attending high school and boarding with two of my sisters – Verna and June. We shared the household chores, and my task was to empty the water pan under the icebox. (If you don't know what an icebox is, ask someone with gray hair.) I didn't always remember, and that became a minor irritant in our otherwise calm and tranquil household – well, as calm and tranquil as any household with two lively young women and their teenage brother might be.

Morning was not Verna's best time either. One morning she walked into the kitchen and went "backside over bumbershoot" in the water that covered the floor. I was sleeping as only teenagers can sleep at that moment, so again, I do not know the exact words Verna said. But they were probably no more reportable than Bev's. All I know is that Verna took that huge basin of ice-water, carried it into my bedroom and unceremoniously dumped the whole thing on my poor, innocent little head.

So as Bev stood poised with that can of water over my nose, I had a flashback, and the flashback combined with the look on her face found me making promises I should have considered more carefully.

So before even getting dressed I stuck my head under the sink. There was the offending drip, and it was obvious that if I tightened that nut, the drip would stop. Except this was an old house with an old tap and one quick turn of that nut broke off the rusty bottom of the tap sending a small squirt of brown water onto my face and plunging our family into crisis.

This was a school day. A work day. All of us had to be out of the house in less than an hour, and the water was shut off because "Dad did something stupid under the sink." We obviously survived, though the details have been mercifully blotted from my memory. I begged off early from work to get home to fix the sink because we couldn't afford a plumber. "Plumbers charge more than brain surgeons," I said to Bev who had suggested it.

On the way home I bought a new set of taps. "Standard size," said the man at the store. Except this standard size didn't fit our unstandard sink and after several trips back and forth it was determined that we would need to replace our vintage sink for which there were no longer any taps.

All this took several hours, by which time the family was all home again, and a strange pall of silence had settled over the house, except for my occasional clanging and banging in the kitchen between trips to the hardware store. "Think of it this way," I said in my most cheerful voice, "We're getting to know our neighbors!"

"The neighbors," said Bev, "are putting 'For Sale' signs on their lawns."

Have you noticed how in life, one things leads to another? Everything is connected. The sink, for instance, was connected to the countertop so that had to be replaced. And the countertop was connected to the kitchen cabinets so those got rebuilt. That left a big gaping bare spot in the linoleum.

We wound up with a brand new kitchen and a debt that took us a year to pay off. Bev started to say something about calling a plumber next time, but tactfully stopped in mid-sentence.

Over the next couple of weeks we invited all the neighbors over for supper. We'd invaded their bathrooms and borrowed their tools, so it was only right we show them why. They were all really fine people, and, it turned out, really glad to help. The one "For Sale" sign had to do with an office transfer, not with us.

We were in trouble. We needed help. We got it. A new kitchen and some new friends.

Everything is connected. It all worked out in the end.

"But next time we call a plumber," says Bev.

Will You Be My Valentine

Not long ago, Bev officiated at a wedding which made the local newspaper, it was so unusual. Not only were both parents of both the bride and groom there, but all eight grandparents as well. And all of them still married to each other.

Even just having all four parents still married to each other is unusual these days. Clergy and others who do weddings know that figuring out the complex relationships of various parents, step-parents and siblings and ex-spouses needs a computer. Or a wizard. And the emotions involved in this changing morality and "family" structure defy understanding. A lively sense of humor becomes the minister's most valuable asset.

One minister told me about a wedding guest who offered a caustic remark at the reception. "The nerve of the bride wearing white. They've been living together for a year. White is a symbol of virginity."

"Of course," said the minister. "She's what's known as a new revised standard virgin."

The hoary headed among us think fondly of the days when couples got married and then had sex. Yes, boys and girls, that's the way it used to be. In those wonderful days, moms and dads never quarreled, and they never got divorced, and all the church pews were filled with happy couples, each with 2.5 kids sitting between them.

Well, a little research and common sense tells us those "good ole days" never did exist. We can't keep the blinkers on anymore.

In our congregation, a couple with three lovely children lit the candles at the beginning of the service last week. Afterward, the father told me, "I was thinking – while we were up there – we're probably the only traditional family left in this congregation." A "normal" family is no longer normal.

All of that stuff was going through my cluttered mind in February while I wondered who I might send a Valentine to this year. A Valentine is a card you send to someone who particularly needs to hear an expression of love, preferably from someone who isn't required to love them. As a child, I got Valentines from my sisters but they were "yucky" and didn't really count because my mother made them do it. But I remember a girl named Carol Spicer (her real name) who was in my class in grade three in Ottawa during the two years we lived there. She was wonderfully beautiful, and I was totally in love with her, and would have died to have received a Valentine from her. She never spoke to me nor I to her. An unrequited love. Sigh!

But if I can't send a Valentine to her, maybe I might find some folks who would really appreciate it on this day when we celebrate romantic bliss. Perhaps to someone who lives with verbal or physical abuse, to the recently divorced and the never married, to gays and lesbians, to teenagers wondering where they belong. And yes, even to the beautiful family with mom and dad and three kids who come up to light the candle. They need love too.

Platitudes don't work anymore, if they ever did. Romantic movies that fade to black on the first kiss don't convince us. The beautiful girl and the handsome boy no longer walk hand in hand into the sunset.

Truth and grace are so hard to articulate. Somehow the sentimentality of Valentine's Day has to be translated into an awareness of God's abundant love expressed in an inclusive community.

Which is so easy to say and so hard to do.

My Valentine for you, in whatever pain you are suffering at the moment, is a wish that you may know love. Not just love in the abstract but genuine love from a real flesh and blood person.

I know. Not everybody can find that. Not even most people. But everybody *needs* that and everybody *deserves* that.

A Bop on the Nose

You've heard the story of the guy who fell off a 50 story skyscraper? On his way past the 25th floor, somebody calls out the window, "Do you need any help?"

"No, thanks. I've gone 25 floors and nothing has happened to me so far. I'm okay."

We men are particularly good at this. Okay, I'll be honest. *I* am particularly good at avoiding problems until they whack me on the proboscis, and then wondering why nobody prepared me for this, conveniently forgetting that people have been trying to do just that.

Twice in my life I have thought of myself as the perfect parent. The first time was just before our first child was born, and I was fantasizing how wonderful I was going to be as a dad. Nobody was going to be more nurturing, more kind, more understanding. I had read Dr. Spock and several articles in the *Reader's Digest* about how to be a good papa, and I just knew I was going to do it all.

The second time didn't last quite as long. It was just before my first grandchild was born and I fantasized myself as the perfect grandparent. There isn't quite as much stuff to read about grandparenting (there should be more), but I had found one book and I read it from cover to cover and I just knew I was going to do it all and do it right. It took maybe 15 seconds for a quibbling voice in my head to say, "Ralph, you didn't quite manage perfection as a father. What makes you think you can manage perfection as a grandfather?"

One of the things I have in my grandfatherly armamentarium that I didn't have as a dad is Meg Hickling's delightful book, *Speaking of Sex*. It's a book that is both very hard and wonderfully easy to read. It's hard, because as a young father, I was the essence of informed liberality, open and clear and scientific about things sexual. Except that as I read Meg's book I keep tripping over the areas I avoided, the things I didn't know and (most surprising) the stuff I find embarrassing. The book is easy to read because Meg explains things so a seven-year-old can understand and that almost includes grandpas.

What brought me up short is Meg's very clear statement that not giving your kids a good and factual grounding in matters sexual makes them vulnerable to sexual predators. It's not just a matter of "street-proofing" kids by telling them about dirty old men in raincoats, but giving them the words and the freedom to talk to mom about Uncle Harry who gets a little too affectionate. Teenagers who are ignorant and confused about sex are far more likely to be promiscuous or find themselves as teenage parents.

There's probably no area of our lives that gives us as much trouble and about which we know so little. It's lots of fun to laugh at kids and the wonderfully strange ideas they get. Like the young man who told Meg that you couldn't get a girl pregnant if you soaked your penis in Coke. The mental picture of that kid with his weenie in a fizzing glass had me laughing for hours. Not as hilarious, but just as serious is that I didn't know very young children can be sexually aroused watching erotic scenes on TV.

I do remember the time when personal matters like sex and bodily functions could be wonderfully, skillfully avoided. For years, as a child, I wondered what those packages of white things were that my sisters hid at the top of their closets. They called them "cornflakes." I didn't really know much about menstruation until after Bev and I were married, except that it was ugly and awful.

What I mostly didn't know about was alternate sexuality. I shudder at the memory of things my buddies and I said about friends who were "queer" or "fruits." None of us had any clear idea what that meant, and it wasn't actually until the last 20 years or so that I actually knew and became friends with gay and lesbian men and women. Correction. I am sure I knew homosexual men and women long before that, but I didn't know they were homosexual.

The time comes when we have to do some clear thinking about our own sexuality, and about the values we attach to this. In just about every family, a son or grandchild will announce that he's gay, a daughter will confront Dad on his sexist attitudes, or one of the children will blow the whistle on the abuse that's there in the family.

We may have to take a long, hard and painful look at some deeply held convictions and values which might not be working anymore. For me, the biggest struggle has been to understand what it means to be a man. Male. I won't take up your time here to talk about that since I've already written a whole book on the subject (*Man to Man*) but it shook me right down to my masculine toenails.

If some of this rethinking hasn't happened in your life or in your family yet, it may be that you are either extremely lucky, or you're better at hiding it than most.

As a parent, I didn't really have a choice about whether my adult sex education would happen. I only had a choice about whether I'd be ready and willing to hear it. And to keep on loving right through to the other side of whatever it is that has to be worked through.

Now, I'm starting to learn all over again about what all this means to me as a grandparent.

Simple Gifts

From a distance it looked jet black, but as we moved closer, the glint of sun revealed a deep navy blue. A single gold stripe, and just a touch of gilt around the portholes revealed the quiet elegance of the Royal Yacht Britannia. It was the little things that added dignity and grace to what is otherwise a very ordinary ship.

Bev and I had walked from our hotel in Toronto to see this legendary ship. "Is it open to the public at any point?" I asked the sailor at the top of the gangplank.

"I'm afraid not, sir," said the sailor.

Back at our hotel, I asked the man at the desk about buses to the airport. "Here's the schedule." He dropped a folder unceremoniously on the counter.

On the flight back home, the flight attendant asked about our meal trays. "Are you guys finished with this?"

Effective communication in all three cases. But from the sailor on the yacht, a subtle but important difference. "I'm afraid not," implied that he sympathized with my request, and "sir" was a term of respect.

I have no idea whether he meant it. It doesn't matter. It was one of those small social graces that helps just a little to make a harsh world more gentle.

When Jim and I have lunch together we often go to a pub and by force of habit sit at the same table. The first time a new waitress came up she very cheerfully asked, "What'll it be, sweetheart."

"I haven't decided yet, my dearest darling," I bristled.

She was taken aback. Offended. I explained to her that since we had never met before, I didn't feel that such terms of endearment were appropriate.

"I didn't mean nothin' by it!" she pouted.

"Exactly." I don't think she understood, and Jim felt I had been a bit abusive. "She's had a long day and doesn't need your lecture on political correctness." Jim was right.

My daughter Grace waited on tables for awhile, and told me, "Dad, you have no idea how a succession of cranky customers can make you feel about two inches high by the end of the day."

It's such a small thing. But recognizing that boarding the Royal Yacht might really be important to Bev and me – or that being called a "guy" feels like a put-down to many women – or being addressed as "sweetheart" feels condescending to many men – recognizing that is a small thing to ask. Whether we agree or not – whether we mean it or not – it's a small gift of consideration and respect we can all afford to give.

Nor is it too much to ask that I understand why the man behind the counter tossed that pamphlet at me. He may have been on his feet all day and maybe his back hurt. He may just have had a phone call from a teenager acting out again. Simple understanding is another small gift we can all afford to give.

It won't change the face of history. But just a bit of thoughtfulness about the folks we meet in the course of our day may help to smooth a life already raw with sharpened edges. Courtesy is a small gift, a simple gift.

It's the little things, the subtle shades of attitude, that make the difference between a Royal Yacht and just another boat – between a civilization and just a bunch of people.

A Gentle, Holy Chuckle

As miracles go, it doesn't rank with the parting of the Red Sea or changing water into wine. But do you remember the broken biffy aboard one of the first US space shuttle flights? I think it was a miracle. A very small one, but a miracle still.

Because some miracles are about God giving us a wink and a gentle poke in the ribs, and in the process, the spiritual gift of laughter.

Every once in a while, when we humans, either individually or collectively, get swelled heads, something happens that reminds us. We are human. We mess up. And if we're lucky, we can laugh about it.

The American people are justifiably proud of the technological accomplishment involved in the space shuttle. They should be. But it seemed to be a bit of divine poetic justice when those superbly trained astronauts, in a billion dollar craft, had to contend with a busted biffy.

"God has put down the mighty from their thrones!" said Mary (Jesus' mother) in the Bible. The mighty astronauts were put down from their throne, so to speak, while the whole world giggled.

I'll bet God giggled too.

• • •

After I'd been boasting to Bev about a new promotion, my teenage daughter (who had been listening with very mild interest) walked up behind my chair, ran her finger around the edge of my bald spot, and said, "Dad, you've got a hole in your head."

I don't think my daughter was trying to bring me back down to earth, though she did exactly that.

I think God had a chuckle over it, and a few days later I did too. I wonder if God created teenage daughters to keep their dads' feet on the ground.

• • •

"An audio-visual expert from New York," the woman called me. It was at a prestigious conference in Chicago. We were in one of those big old churches, the kind with the long center aisle slanting down to the front – the kind brides love to walk down. We were to see a film, but the projectionist didn't show. The woman in charge of the program asked me if I could run a projector. After all, I was there representing a media consulting outfit from New York.

"A piece of cake," I said. "Sure."

Hundreds of people had gathered and were waiting. The church was full. To fill time while I threaded the projector, the woman went up to the pulpit and said how grateful they were to have the "audio visual expert from New York" to help them out. She used that phrase several times. And I'd be lying if I said I didn't enjoy it.

Well – you know that little toggle thing on the front reel of a movie projector – the one that holds the full roll of film in place?

The lights went off, the projector came on, and the front roll of film flipped off with a great clatter and unrolled all the way down the long, sloping aisle to the front.

I turned the projector off and the lights came on just in time to show a red-faced audio visual expert from New York winding up the film from the front of the church to the back.

Following the film, there was a closing meditation. The scripture? You guessed it. Mary's poem, from the Bible. "God has put down the mighty from their thrones. . . ."

Lying on my hotel room bed that night, my face still burning with embarrassment, I could hear, in the darkness around me, a soft and loving chuckle.

• • •

If you had attended the Canadian Bible Society annual dinner in Winnipeg back in 1961, you would have heard me make a speech. "The printed word is *passé*, and books as such will be unknown in a decade," I intoned. I thought I was being prophetic. A few others must have thought so too, because the speech was printed in five magazines in three countries.

Now, almost four decades later, having founded and retired from a large publishing company*, this writer of books feels himself again, embraced by a gentle, holy, chuckle.

*Northstone Publishing and Wood Lake Books

Growing Beauty in the Manure

I grew the pumpkin in manure. Well, a mixture of manure and compost and soil in a large heap. Just for the heck of it.

I ordered the pumpkin seeds specially. They weren't pumpkins, technically, but a variety of squash. Hey, they were large and orange and who would know? They were called "giant" and came from some of those huge "pumpkins" people put in competitions.

I planted several seeds in my well-rotted manure pile. Then, as they sprouted and grew, I clipped away the weakest plants first, then the smallest blossoms, then the smallest forming pumpkin, until all the energy, all the "good" of that stinking pile was channeled into my one pumpkin.

It was huge. It took three of us to lift it into a wheelbarrow, then into the back of a pickup truck, then into the church for Thanksgiving where it sat, dwarfing the communion table, dwarfing everything. In fact Bev, who was the minister of the church, raised a few liturgical eyebrows at the whole business, but by this time there was a gaggle of parishioners admiring my monstrosity and people saying, "I've got to tell my uncle to come to church on Sunday – he's got to see this." What could she do?

To say the pumpkin dominated the church and the worship service would be too much of an understatement. In the scheme of things, especially in hindsight, it was not a good idea. It will go down in history as "The year Ralph brought in that humungous pumpkin."

I don't remember the sermon Bev preached, and probably most of the rest of the folks didn't either. The sermon I preached in my own head was a thanksgiving for the wonder that grows out of the refuse, the compost, the manure of our lives. God can turn the stinkiest stuff into beauty and grandeur.

After the service, I found myself talking to a very unhappy family. Dad had left. Permanently it seems. Mom was having a hard time coping. Bev was working with them and helping them through the crisis, but on the spur of the moment, I gave them the pumpkin. It was delivered by the same strong-backed trio in a pickup who brought it to the church.

"It was exactly what we needed," said the mother in that sad family a month or two later. "We spent Thanksgiving Day cutting up that monster. With a saw and an ax! We'll be eating squash forever. But for that moment, during those first few days after my husband walked out on us, it gave us something to laugh about, to be happy about, and to do together. Thanks."

Good things can grow in manure.

I Don't Like Thanksgiving

I was at a wedding a few weeks ago.

The couple was radiantly happy. There were prayers of thanksgiving in the service, there were speeches and toasts at the reception, all of them delighting in the celebration of a covenant.

At the wedding was the groom's older sister. Her marriage had come apart a few weeks earlier. I caught a glimpse of tears in her eyes during the reception, and because we had been friends for many years, I invited her to dance and asked her how she was making out. "Does it seem a little unfair?" I asked.

The question surprised her. "No. Not unfair. It's painful, of course. But it's not unfair. In fact, I can rejoice with my brother at a deeper level because I also know the flip side of all this."

I have problems every Thanksgiving when the chancel of our church is loaded with garden produce. I have problems because I'm not convinced garden produce is a suitable symbol any longer. It has more to do with nostalgia than with thanksgiving. Nostalgia for the good old days, and thanksgiving are two very different things.

I have problems because so much of our thanksgiving celebration has to do with denying pain. "Hey, this is Thanksgiving day. Forget all the crappy stuff and celebrate." Well, no, because genuine thanksgiving always takes place in the *context* of pain.

Earlier in the year, I blubbered all through the wedding of my daughter Kari. I cried with joy, of course, but I also cried because I know the pain and the struggle and the heartache they will have to face, if their relationship is to be genuine and life-giving.

One of my favorite Bible stories is about Mary and Joseph taking their little baby Jesus to the temple. It was customary to make an offering on behalf of the first-born son, and being good Jews, Mary and Joseph wanted to do the right thing. But in the temple, they encountered an old man named Simeon. He picked up the baby Jesus and expressed his thanks and joy. Then he looked deeply into Mary's eyes and said, "a sword will pierce your heart."

Old Simeon couldn't predict the future. He could have said those words to any mother. Every parent knows that children bring both joy and pain and that you don't have one without the other.

In fact, one may not be possible without the other. Is it possible to have joy without having known pain first? It seems to me, thanksgiving has to do with accepting, yes even appreciating the pain that comes with life, as well as the joy.

Genuine thanksgiving grows in the pain and refuse of our lives.

As If

The first phone call came at 9 this morning. The son of our friends had an aneurysm. He was in critical condition in hospital. Two hours later a second phone call. He was on life-support. There was no hope.

"For God's sake, God, what are you up to? The kid just got out of school. His life was just beginning. He was a good kid, a bright kid, an active kid, with his whole life in front of him. His parents and his family loved him. What the hell do you think you're doing taking him like that? Why?"

My angry mind goes back to a bedside where my nephew Jay is dying of cancer. A priest comes and anoints his dying friend. There are tears in his eyes as he reads an ancient lament from a well-worn book. I walk down the hall with the priest to the hospital lounge and we sit there for a long while without words.

"He was my friend," says the priest. "He sang in our choir." He rubs the pain behind his eyes. "It's not so bad when they are old and have had a full life. But his life was just beginning, and I wish to hell I understood why he had to die."

I take the man's hand, and the tears in our eyes allow us to be pastor to each other.

I have a letter written by Jim Taylor who lost his son Stephen from cystic fibrosis. He didn't write the letter to me. He wrote the letter to...well to God maybe, or to himself. He wrote a lot of letters in his grief, letters of pain and rage and frustration and fear. That huge, eternal, unanswerable "Why?" screams out of them.

The letter that I have, somewhat rumpled from re-reading, offers no answer to that "Why?" It is a question as old as Job and as raw as a festering, open wound. Perhaps it isn't even a question as much as it is a protest against what seems so futile and meaningless and vindictive and random and cruel.

Jim's letter talks about choices. When he and Joan found out about Stephen's cystic fibrosis, they could have plunged themselves into despair and simply given up. But, as Jim says, they chose to live as if...

As if Stephen's life mattered.

As if God was a loving God who loved all of them and cried with them in their pain.

As if love and joy were life's reality, not pain and death.

They chose to live that way, and because they made that choice, they now see Stephen's life as a gift. Of course, they would do anything to have him back, but they are now, years after his death, finally able to feel thanks for the time they had together, for the memories, for the spirit that is still there and part of their lives.

It took ten years of tears and struggle, but Jim's letter, and many other letters came together into a remarkable book. It's called *Letters to Stephen* and I have given copies to many friends and family in their grieving.

The friends who lost their son today won't read that book for several years, even though they are Jim's friends too and probably have an autographed copy. But they can't read it now. Now, if they come upon it, they must throw it in the corner in their rage.

Before there can be healing, there must be tears and anger and depression. But then they will eventually learn to live as if...

As if life really matters.

As if their son's life mattered.

As if God is a loving God who loves them and cries with them in their pain.

As if love and joy are life's reality, not pain and death.

At first it will be just going through the motions. At first it will feel phony and wrong. But then, living as if God's love is there, the pretense will become the reality.

When we have no answers, we must live as if we do.

And then, in time, we will.

• • •

I wrote those words only a few weeks before we got that terrible phone call from Grace. "The police called. They found Lloyd's body..."

There are many places in this book where I've left myself vulnerable. Naked. Now I simply feel helpless. I have no words. I have tried to write about this, to reflect on it, and in time I will.

But not now.

282 • Angels in Red Suspenders

Now, all I can do is share the letter which we wrote as a family to friends in many places – some who had already heard through the grapevine, and some who had not heard.

• • •

Dear friends,

Many of you have heard that our son Lloyd died on May 4th. Others may not be aware of this tragic news. This is an open letter to all of you, because it is impossible for us, at this time, to respond to each of you individually.

Lloyd's death was a terrible shock to all of us, but most particularly to his twin sister, Grace. But as we gathered a small group of family around us in a little memorial service to say good-bye to Lloyd, Grace told the story of a remarkable dream she'd had – a dream that ministered to all of us.

To appreciate the meaning of the dream, you need to know that Lloyd had never known how to give or receive affection. The fetal alcohol syndrome he suffered at birth and the abuse of his first two years in a foster home made it impossible for him to know that he was loved, or that he had been endowed with many gifts.

In the dream, Lloyd had been sitting with Grace on the edge of her bed, and giving her a big hug. "Then he said, 'I have found our father.' At first I thought he meant our birth father, but then I realized he meant God."

At the end of our memorial service, we heard a tape of a pianist playing *The Rose*. Lloyd had a gift of music, but could not believe the gift, and so didn't develop it. But he loved that song, perhaps because it spoke of the potential so many of us saw in him, of the "seed" that, it seems, needed to die beneath the snows so that somehow, somewhere, it can blossom "with the sun's love" into a rose.

We ache with the loss of our son, and wish he could have changed his last and final choice. But it was his. And we know that Lloyd has learned how to love, and that he has found God. The rose has blossomed. We are in pain, but we are at peace.

Some have asked what they can do to remember Lloyd, and we have suggested that money be given to the Healing Fund of the United Church of Canada. This fund goes to First Nations people to help them heal the social and spiritual wounds they have suffered. It's too late to help Lloyd, but the fund may prevent his kind of suffering for some other children.

We are grateful and overwhelmed by the outpouring of love and care that has come to us. Folks from coast to coast have written – there were notes from childhood friends we have not seen for 40 years – some from folk we do not even know personally.

As you know, grief takes its physical, emotional and spiritual toll, and we simply cannot respond individually to each of you. We know you understand, and will accept this as our thanks.

Yours with love,
Bev & Ralph Milton

• • •

And so we live as if...
For now, it is enough.